CURRICULUM
mapping

P9-AQB-830

To my parents, Sid and Charlene Tuchman,
who always believed I could accomplish whatever I set my mind to do

CURRICULUM
mapping

A Step-by-Step Guide for
Creating Curriculum Year Overviews

MONTGOMERY COUNTY PUBLIC SCHOOLS
PROFESSIONAL LIBRARY
850 HUNGERFORD DRIVE
ROCKVILLE, MARYLAND 20850

WITHDRAWN

kathy tuchman glass

FOREWORD BY BENA KALLICK

CORWIN PRESS
A SAGE Publications Company
Thousand Oaks, CA 91320

JAN 1 0 2007

Copyright © 2007 by Corwin Press

All rights reserved. When forms and sample documents are included, their use is authorized only by educators, local school sites, and/or noncommercial entities who have purchased the book. Except for that usage, no part of this book may be reproduced or utilized in any form or by any means, electronic or mechanical, including photocopying, recording, or by any information storage and retrieval system, without permission in writing from the publisher.

Standards and Benchmarks used throughout the book are from Marzano, Robert, Kendall, John (2004). *Content Knowledge: A Compendium of Standards and Benchmarks for K–12 Education*, 4th ed. Aurora, CO: McREL. Copyright 2004, McREL. Used and/or adapted by permission of McREL.

For information:

Corwin Press
A Sage Publications Company
2455 Teller Road
Thousand Oaks, California 91320
www.corwinpress.com

Sage Publications Ltd.
1 Oliver's Yard
55 City Road
London EC1Y 1SP
United Kingdom

Sage Publications India Pvt. Ltd.
B-42, Panchsheel Enclave
Post Box 4109
New Delhi 110 017 India

Printed in the United States of America.

Library of Congress Cataloging-in-Publication Data

Glass, Kathy Tuchman.
Curriculum mapping: A step-by-step guide for creating curriculum year overviews / Kathy Tuchman Glass.
       p. cm.
Includes bibliographical references and index.
ISBN 1-4129-1558-9 or 978-1-412915-58-8 (cloth)
ISBN 1-4129-1559-7 or 978-1-412915-59-5 (pbk.)
    1. Curriculum planning. 2. Curriculum evaluation. 3. Teacher participation in curriculum planning. I. Title.
LB2806.15.G565 2007
375.001—dc22   2006019602

This book is printed on acid-free paper.

06   07   08   09   10   11   9   8   7   6   5   4   3   2   1

Acquisitions Editors:	Kylee Liegl and Allyson P. Sharp
Editorial Assistant:	Nadia Kashper
Production Editor:	Diane S. Foster
Copy Editor:	Bill Bowers
Typesetter:	C&M Digitals (P) Ltd.
Proofreader:	Christine Dahlin
Indexer:	Kristen Kite
Cover Designer:	Scott Van Atta
Graphic Designer:	Lisa Riley

Contents

List of Figures

Foreword

Curriculum mapping has been sweeping the country. Many districts are focusing on mapping as a method for keeping the curriculum dynamic in an age in which much is changing—standards change, students change, state assessments change, and, most significantly, we teachers are continuously growing, learning, and changing.

This book provides a window into how Kathy Glass has developed a system for mapping that enhances the traditional model. She suggests that we can map with a year overview in mind—one in which mapping can be done across subjects and as a developmental continuum. Her careful explanations leave the reader with not only a step-by-step guide but also excellent examples of the types of maps that she is suggesting.

There are many mapping paths that we can take—as long as they all take us in the same direction—to provide a curriculum that is focused on improving student learning. This book, in combination with the other books that she has referenced, provides a strong foundation for curriculum and instruction.

In addition to her focus on curriculum mapping, she has included some valuable tips on how to build a professional learning community. Mapping is at the heart of professional learning communities. When teachers map, they are documenting the journey their students will be taking or have already taken from the beginning of school to the end. Although it is helpful for teachers to document such journeys because it provides a basis for thoughtful planning and reflection, part of the power of these documents is that collectively they tell a story of the curriculum students have been addressing in a school year. And, as mapping continues, the story unfolds across grades, buildings, departments, and finally, creates a systemwide picture.

This sort of picture was extremely difficult to portray before we had easy access to technology. Now, rather than having dozens of file folders and papers stored in file cabinets and piled on desks, it is possible to have a Web-based software application that not only provides a library of maps but also summarizes and organizes the data that has been entered into reports that serve as a catalyst for professional conversations.

Kathy shares her enthusiasm for the discoveries that she has made both by mapping and by coaching others in the mapping process.

—Bena Kallick
Educational Consultant and
Vice-President of Performance Pathways

Acknowledgments

I thank the following teachers, whose collaboration helped me refine my work with curriculum mapping and articulation. Teachers in the following school districts enthusiastically embraced our work together to better hone their craft. In the process of guiding them, I grew immeasurably.

Abbott, Bayside, and Bowditch Middle Schools (San Mateo–Foster City School District, San Mateo, CA)

McKinley Elementary School (Burlingame Elementary School District, Burlingame, CA)

Oak Knoll, Laurel, and Encinal Elementary Schools (Menlo Park City School District, Menlo Park, CA)

Ormondale Elementary School and Corte Madera School (Portola Valley School District, Portola Valley, CA)

Ronald C. Wornick Jewish Day School (Foster City, CA)

Woodside Elementary School District (Woodside, CA)

I thank those who carefully reviewed my manuscripts. These educators offered keen insight and comments that provided meaningful guidance:

Johnna Becker
Fourth-Grade Teacher
Oak Knoll Elementary School
Menlo Park, CA

Robert Boram
Professor of Science
Morehead State University
Morehead, KY

Margo Gibson
Principal
Jemison High School
Jemison, AL

Cynthia Givens
Director, The Education Station
Laramie County School District
Number One
Cheyenne, WY

Constance L. Hill
Teacher Specialist
South Carolina Department of Education
Columbia, SC

Karen I. Hughes
Classroom Teacher (English,
Speech, Drama)
Nashville High School
Nashville, AR

Kim Newlove
Superintendent of Education
Saskatoon Public Schools
Saskatoon, Saskatchewan,
Canada

Jamie Jahnig
English Teacher
Central High School
Cheyenne, WY

Rodney Rich
Principal
Calabasas Middle School
Rio Rico, AZ

Joseph Meersman
Video Production Instructor
Toppenish High School
Toppenish, WA

My editors, Kylee Liegl and Allyson Sharp, once again deserve my genuine appreciation for championing this project. I am grateful for their ongoing support and kind hearts.

Of course, these acknowledgments would not be complete without thanking those closest to me. My husband, Mike, is forever willing to do his part and then some. Without him, I truly could not have managed to write this book. My children, Kimberly and Marshall, take pride in my work, as I do in theirs. Their support is what helps to fuel my passion for writing.

About the Author

 **Kathy Tuchman Glass,** a former teacher and master teacher who holds current teaching certification, now consults at schools and districts, presents at conferences, and teaches seminars for university and county programs to customize and deliver professional development. She works with a myriad of teachers from newcomers to veterans—from one-on-one to whole staff or district—in areas affecting curriculum and instruction. By assisting administrators and teachers with strategic planning to determine school and district objectives, she focuses on various topics, such as curriculum design, interdisciplinary teaching, instructional strategies, six traits of writing, differentiated instruction, curriculum mapping, and more.

During her 17 years in education, she has also been involved in publishing. In addition to *Curriculum Mapping: A Step-by-Step Guide to Creating Curriculum Year Overviews,* she wrote *Curriculum Design for Writing Instruction: Creating Standards-Based Lesson Plans and Rubrics* (copyright 2005, Corwin Press; foreword by Carol Ann Tomlinson). Currently she is working on a project for the Parallel Curriculum Model with Carol Ann Tomlinson and the model's other authors. Previously she served as contributing writer and consultant for the Heath Middle Level Literature series (copyright 1995, DC Heath and Company).

Originally from Indianapolis, Indiana, Kathy now resides in the San Francisco Bay Area with her supportive husband and two loving children. She can be contacted by e-mail at kathy@kathyglassconsulting.com or through her Web site at www.kathyglassconsulting.com.

Introduction

Hollywood played an instrumental role in fueling my passion for teaching. While eating popcorn and watching films that mesmerized me, such as *To Sir With Love, Stand and Deliver,* and *The Sound of Music,* I imagined myself in the protagonists' roles imparting youth with knowledge and serving as their catalyst for positive growth. Additionally, at 16, my mother—co-owner of a private career counseling business—administered a computer-generated test that included a possibility from among several hundred vocational options. My future targeted direction result: ENGLISH TEACHER.

After a detour from graduation to advertising on Madison Avenue, I could not deny my innate calling to help inspire young minds. A decade after the test-taking, I traded the promising advertising career for another stint at college to earn a teaching credential and later a master's degree. It was with this newfound career that I learned the true definition of having a passion for work. To that point, I had not understood the advertising man's yen for pulling late nights at the office or catching the subway to work before I was fully awake. Once I was teaching classes and volunteering in the classroom, though, the passion struck me and fueled my desire to grow professionally each month, each year, even now.

When I secured my first teaching position in early summer, I left the principal's office laden with textbooks for subjects I would teach. (Even though I was weighted down by the voluminous texts, I had an energetic bounce in my step.) I spent that summer planning lessons to prepare myself for the school year. With a bent for lesson planning, I filled several file cabinet drawers and felt amply prepared to begin with my newfound calling.

Reflecting upon my first year teaching, though, I realized it was lacking an overarching organizational structure. I did not receive standards to guide my instruction, and I sometimes felt anxious about what my next unit of instruction would be. I felt that most lessons I taught were meaningful and student achievement increased, but I knew viscerally that there was a way I could service my student-clients much better. It was later in my career that I learned to use standards to help guide my teaching as one significant step to being a better teacher.

After teaching for many years, I transitioned into consulting. As a consultant, I provide various curriculum and instruction workshops, coaching, and support to various audiences (i.e., conference attendees, districts, school site staffs, grade level groups, individual teachers) on a number of topics. I am continually working to meet the needs of my teacher-clients, which gave rise to my work with what I call a Curriculum Year Overview (CYO). Long ago, I thought about what I could provide to assist teachers and move them ahead along the professional continuum. I collaborated with teachers to create standards-based units, facilitate scoring writing assessments, and offer other professional materials and services, but what I came to realize was that something was needed to tie all the pieces together. The curriculum and instructional support were not meant to be used in isolation; they demanded a thread to provide cohesion. It was then that I thought my clients might benefit from a document that shows connections between and continuity among the standards-based units of study and augmented by assessments, skills, guiding questions, resources, and teacher instructional notes to personalize standards and outline units of study. I then collaborated with teachers to create an overarching, year-long plan that I have always called a CYO.

It was not until later that I discovered the work of Heidi Hayes Jacobs and realized that a CYO actually *was* a curriculum map. In her book *Getting Results with Curriculum Mapping,* Jacobs (2004) defines curriculum mapping as "a procedure for collecting data about the operational curriculum in a school or district referenced directly to the calendar." The aim of this book is to guide teachers to develop what is included in the actual maps: *unit guiding questions, standards, skills, resources,* and *assessments.* The distinction between this book and others on curriculum mapping rests largely on the procedure of creating the finished map. Therefore, I use the terms CYO and curriculum mapping interchangeably. So, if you are already familiar with curriculum mapping, this book will elaborate upon the process and enhance what you have already been doing in this area. If you are new to curriculum mapping, this book offers you a detailed step-by-step approach to create this kind of document.

I well know that what I present to you in this book rests on the work of giants in the field of education, including Heidi Hayes Jacobs, Lynn Erickson, Jay McTighe, and Grant Wiggins. Heidi Hayes Jacobs is especially noteworthy, as she has been at the forefront of curriculum mapping. Her book *Getting Results with Curriculum Mapping* will provide further insight for those embarking upon curriculum mapping projects. It would also behoove those serious about curriculum mapping to read her earlier book *Mapping the Big Picture: Integrating Curriculum & Assessment K–12* (1997), as well as *Keys to Curriculum Mapping: Strategies and Tools to Make It Work* by Susan Udelhofen (2005).

Lynn Erickson has helped me think deeply about concept-based learning and designing a curriculum that is not fact and activity driven. My copy of her book *Concept-Based Curriculum and Instruction* is dog-eared and slightly battered after much use, as I refer to it often when designing meaningful curriculum for students. It will allow you, as facilitator, to supplement the discussion of concepts, standards, skills, and more with what you have learned from Lynn Erickson. Authors Jay McTighe and Grant Wiggins (2005) have played a pivotal role in the world of education and have contributed to my knowledge base as well. Their book *Understanding by Design* provides teachers with a framework and design process from which they can plan units that elicit more understanding from students.

All those mentioned have made significant contributions to the thoughtful work of providing a rationale, and defining and developing essential questions. I have gleaned much from the work of these authors as they have further enhanced my growth as a professional and will no doubt for you, too, as you supplement your learning. If you want to do additional reading, I strongly encourage you to peruse the Bibliography section and obtain books written by these and other authors listed.

This book is intended to guide facilitators in assisting teachers to map out their school year with an articulated game plan to follow as they meticulously educate and steer students. In this book, I will:

- Define in detail a Curriculum Year Overview (CYO)—or curriculum map.
- List the purposes.
- Delineate what one can include.
- Explain the step-by-step process for creating a Curriculum Year Overview.
- Share suggestions for articulation.
- Provide numerous sample CYOs.

Think of a menu as a metaphor for educational design: the *Curriculum Year Overview* is the basic meal of a protein, a starch, and a vegetable that is the starting point for chefs as they build menus. It is essentially the fundamental outline or framework of any balanced meal, as it provides direction but is not replete with details. The *units referenced in the CYO* represent specific menu items based on the balanced meals, for example, steak and chicken (protein), potato and pasta (starch), plus asparagus and broccoli (vegetable). *Articulation* is reflective in the other menu items added, such as wine, appetizers, and desserts. Finally, the *specific comprehensive units* with detailed lessons are the recipes for the complete meal: beef tenderloin with cabernet sauce; roasted garlic potatoes with rosemary; grilled asparagus with parmesan cheese. It is a chef's job to prepare a full-course meal, knowing that balance is important and using the menu as a guidepost.

I see the work of this curriculum map as the overall balance of a well-rounded menu, which represents the framework and first step. Once food groups are decided, teachers can then determine the types of menu items and specific recipes; i.e., identify curriculum units, articulate across grade levels, and create comprehensive units. These units of instruction are referenced on the curriculum map along with standards, guiding questions, skills, resources, assessments, and teachers' notes so there is a detailed meal plan for finding recipes and cooking. When it is time to begin donning an apron—by creating specific units of study—you will ensure that each unit is planned and prepared properly with objectives, lesson explanations, detailed assessments, and so forth to give it the depth and dimension for teaching and learning.

I believe that teachers' year-long educational programs will be more cohesive—and their teaching more effective—once units are thoughtfully laid out in the overarching CYO, so there is a sound reason for what is taught and when. Once this is complete, then educators can expand to other courses like appetizers, dessert, and wine and eventually focus on a polished compendium of tested recipes. Expanding to these other course offerings is analogous to working toward articulation and consistency from grade to grade at a school site and district. This will inevitably contribute to successful learning. The more carefully the chef plans a well-rounded menu in which items complement one another, the more satisfied the diners will be because of variety, care in preparation, and optimal taste sensation. All committed professionals evaluate and revise their work accordingly. A chef might add new menu items and delete others based on customer satisfaction or dissatisfaction and availability of ingredients. So is true of a teacher who revisits the CYO and makes changes and revisions based on a variety of factors. Therefore, at various times, you will probably revise menu items and add new recipes along the way.

When considering the audience for this book, I naturally think of teachers as the end-users. But it is more likely that the audience for this text is the educational consultant, district curriculum coordinator, facilitator, or someone in the position of leading a group of teachers on their journey to create curriculum overviews. If you are an individual teacher wanting to write a CYO alone, though, this book will also serve as an exceptional guide to the curriculum mapping process.

1

Definition, Purpose, and Observations

CURRICULUM YEAR OVERVIEW DEFINITION

A Curriculum Year Overview (CYO), or curriculum mapping document, as the name implies, maps everything—in all subject areas—that a teacher needs to cover in a given school year. The CYO accounts for all the content standards the district or state mandates, along with information that personalizes the document for each teacher. This can include resources (such as school-adopted textbooks, a teacher's favorite trade or picture books, software, and so on), interdisciplinary connections, culminating projects or other assessments, guiding questions for the unit, skills to be taught, and so forth. For most elementary school teachers, the CYO must be comprehensive, for it takes into account several subject areas for a self-contained classroom. On the other hand, since a middle or high school teacher is responsible for only one or two subject areas—such as social studies, science, a core class of language arts, social studies, or a similar configuration—the CYO will reflect this. In Chapter 4 are numerous sample CYOs for primary through high school. For some, there is a "year-at-a-glance," which is a list of the representative topics, units of study, skills, and so forth, to provide a cursory look at the school year. All sample CYOs include a comprehensive map of selected monthly units. Participants are directed to these samples at a designated time in the step-by-step process featured in Chapter 2.

Please keep in mind, however, that no two Curriculum Year Overviews will look exactly alike, even for the same grade where students are expected to abide by the same content standards for a school, district, or state. Why? Because teachers have diverse students, use different textbooks and resources, and possess individual teaching styles. The samples included in this book are meant to provide guidance, a starting point, and ideas for content and format as you facilitate an exercise and collaborate with teachers to create a personalized CYO. When the curriculum map is crafted, in addition to mapping standards, identifying skills and assessments, and so forth, it will reflect each teacher's personal flair and individuality, because an essential element of teaching comes from teachers' passion for their profession. Teachers may express their individuality through referencing an effective resource book that is just right, grouping standards in a specific way, citing the perfect piece of art to illustrate a concept, identifying a unique authentic assessment, or naming the guest speaker who enhances learning.

PURPOSES OF A CURRICULUM YEAR OVERVIEW

There are many reasons to create a CYO or curriculum map. Here are some that have inspired me, but you could most likely add to this list your own purposes, which I may have inadvertently omitted. Following this list is an explanation of each purpose, based on my experience working with numerous teacher groups. A CYO can:

1. Provide an outline for the school year.

2. Validate teaching to standards and accountability to using standards as a guide.

3. Identify skills and concepts embedded in standards and craft guiding questions.

4. Reference culminating unit assessments.

5. Provide a comprehensive listing of available resources and materials.

6. Allow for support and consistency in a grade level and foster teamwork.

7. Promote articulation from grade to grade.

8. Serve as a marketing and communications tool.

You might exclaim, "A Curriculum Year Overview does all that?" Well, that is completely up to the teacher group who chooses to create a CYO. I realize that other curriculum maps may address some of these purposes or additional ones. However, for my clients, I propose everything that a Curriculum Year Overview can become. Teachers then decide how comprehensive they want it to be, based on the time they have available, the effort they choose to put into it, the number of subjects they teach and wish to include in the document, the way in which the CYO will be used, and their target audiences (for example, current teachers, future teachers, community members, administrators, and so on).

PURPOSE EXPLANATIONS

Provide an Outline for the School Year

The foremost reason to create a CYO is to provide teachers with a complete outline of what is taught from September to June (or year-round, if the school is configured that way). A seemingly overwhelming number of state or district standards must be covered, so laying out the standards in a way that parallels how teachers deliver curriculum—by thoughtfully placing each standard in a time and situation that has meaning—can assist these professionals in doing their jobs. Additionally, in a CYO teachers not only map content standards, but use them to develop guiding questions, skills, and assessments for curriculum units to be taught, so the final product is a comprehensive outline.

Earlier I provided a metaphor of a chef, but I will now purposely mix metaphors to provide a different vantage point. Essentially, the CYO provides teachers with a curriculum road map for the year. Imagine sightseeing road travelers who originate in San Francisco, wish to reach New York City, and plan to take advantage of main attractions on the way. They would map out their journey so that they reach several milestones while setting their sights on the final destination. As teachers travel along the school year, they are charged with teaching to these milestones in a productive and well-organized manner through June, and the CYO records this journey in detail.

Validate Teaching to Standards and Accountability to Using Standards as a Guide

When I first work with teachers to create a CYO, they seem hesitant and apprehensive when I broach the conversation about which standards they meet and how they meet them. First, I ask them just to talk about what goes on in their classrooms at a certain time of year. After teachers share information about a unit, I take out the standards and point to those that they meet. This validates what they do. Sometimes standards are written in lofty language, or the teachers are not so familiar with each of them, so they are unaware that they are meeting so many standards in their classrooms week in and week out. Teachers beam as they realize that most standards are not so cumbersome, or that they are meeting many more than they originally thought. This moment of self-reflection and affirmation is gratifying, and makes it easier to discuss which standards need further attention or are trouble spots.

In the business world, management by objectives (MBO) is a common way of conducting business. Managers who set objectives are more likely to achieve them than those who do not. Striving to reach an objective without specific or measurable goals is analogous to managing by the seat of your pants. Teaching is no different. Teaching is less effective when teachers haphazardly teach with no standards to guide them.

Peter Drucker (1993), preeminent author of numerous economics publications, editorial columnist for *The Wall Street Journal*, and professor, states in his book *The Practice of Management*, "Setting objectives enables a business to get where it should be going rather than be the plaything of weather, winds, and accidents." In teaching, standards help to set objectives as they provide teachers with a target to shoot for and allow for measurement. One cannot manage or teach effectively what one does not measure. This is an important point to mention to teachers to emphasize the importance of grade-level standards.

Regardless of the knowledge teachers have about standards or their epiphany at covering more standards than they thought, the important by-product of creating a CYO is teachers' realization that they are accountable to teach to district or state standards or other guidelines set forth by the school. In fact, local or state regulations mandate that teachers teach to certain standards. The CYO is also a valuable exercise in uncovering those standards that teachers feel are developmentally inappropriate or determining that some standards might be addressed through colleague collaboration. These valuable conversations about standards set the stage for articulation across grade levels.

Identify Skills and Concepts Embedded in Standards and Craft Guiding Questions

One significant purpose of critically reviewing standards is for teachers to identify key facts, skills, and concepts embedded in them in an effort to be clear-sighted about the overarching objectives and essential understandings of any unit. Additionally, crafting guiding questions allows teachers to be crystal clear about what the essence of instruction involves, so they can focus their learning and guide students. Many standards documents do a fine job of listing facts that students should come to know. However, if teachers were to teach solely a set of isolated facts and details, the students would not glean as much as if they were taught these facts within a conceptual framework. As teachers examine the standards and come to understand these key facts, skills, and overarching concepts and begin to design guiding questions, they will be more informed when plotting standards and their essential information. These key facets will then be used to create, remodel, or find effective curriculum units of instruction so students will receive a sound instructional program.

Reference Culminating Unit Assessments

Good teaching dictates ongoing assessment in a variety of ways throughout the unit, such as informally or formally tracking student participation during classroom discussion, assessing performance on homework and in-class work, and the like. Additionally, at the end of a unit teachers issue an assessment that reflects what students have learned after a comprehensive unit of study. Some teachers call it a culminating project or product, and it is typically authentic, extensive, and differentiated. It might be a writing assignment, a creative project, a lab demonstration, or a performance. The Curriculum Year Overview includes a list of ongoing assessments, as well as the culminating projects. The actual curriculum units will include the comprehensive detail of the activities and accompanying assessments, for if too much detail were included in each CYO, it would be cumbersome and deter teachers from using it. State, school, and district assessments are listed as well.

Provide a Comprehensive Listing of Available Resources and Materials

Included in this yearlong outline is a comprehensive listing of teachers' resources and materials that support specific standards. These can include whatever teachers have at their disposal—resources and materials from colleagues and the school library, a published or teacher-generated unit guide, textbooks, speaker information, and so on. For example, a teacher who conducts a unit on rocks and minerals would enter a catalogue of resources, such as a student science textbook with page and chapter numbers cited, picture book titles, an excerpt from a college text, library book references, Web site links, a reference to a colleague, rock and mineral samples, and field trip information for a local museum. When teachers begin their units of instruction, all resource references are on hand in the CYO so they can prepare appropriately.

Allow for Support and Consistency in a Grade Level and Foster Teamwork

Teachers often move or retire, leaving the school in the position of filling a teaching assignment. Or an experienced teacher changes grade levels and is unfamiliar with the curriculum of the new grade. Presenting new teachers or seasoned teachers who change grades with a Curriculum Year Overview will assist them in their new positions. A CYO decreases the time it takes veteran teachers to apprise the new hires about what is covered in their grades, supports consistency in a grade level, allows all teachers to see new perspectives, and provides much-needed and appreciated support for those beginning a new position that is oftentimes overwhelming.

Because it features a master plan, a CYO can also foster teamwork among job share partners, teachers on an interdisciplinary team, and those who work at the same grade level. In a job share situation, the CYO certainly aids in continuity, since teachers are switching off days, weeks, or even semesters. Most important, in creating a CYO as a job share team, teachers can be in concert with one another philosophically about how they approach units of study; for example, how they group particular standards, craft unit guiding questions, delineate skills, and design assessments.

In an interdisciplinary team, teachers can foster teamwork by planning their units of study to coincide thematically, so students can make connections and further their understanding of concepts. In *The Parallel Curriculum Model (2001)* by Carol Tomlinson et al., the authors propose "developing appropriately challenging curriculum using . . . four 'parallel' ways of thinking about course content." One of the parallels, the Parallel of Connections, leads students to make connections within or across disciplines, times, cultures, or places. When learning is coupled in a meaningful way that fosters connections, the brain is more effective in assimilating and retaining this information. For example, teachers in a team might create a thematic unit for "conflicts" so that in language arts, students read various short stories in which groups of individuals encounter conflicts. In social studies, students study the patterns and causes of various wars. In science, students study chemical warfare or conflicts that stem from a particular scientific topic (e.g., genetically engineered products or environmental issues). Working as an interdisciplinary team, teachers can devise the CYO so these units of study coincide not only thematically, but also in a complementary timeframe so that specific lessons are taught simultaneously to foster connective learning. Also, the guiding questions that team teachers devise serve to make the unit cohesive so that students can see the connections across content areas.

Aside from job sharing and interdisciplinary teams, teachers who work on a grade-level team can also use the CYO to provide consistency among content taught. In communities where parents are highly involved, some teachers say that the CYO helps to satisfy parents' issues or concerns about what is covered from classroom to classroom at the same grade, and even from grade to grade. That said, teachers are not always required to work together to plan what they teach and when they teach it. Teachers in the same grade level can cover standards in different ways, and that works quite well in many schools and allows for flexibility of teachers' styles and interests. Hence, the CYO reflects different teaching approaches but verifies that the same standards are addressed.

Promote Articulation From Grade to Grade

A significant benefit to creating a CYO is to inform teachers about what is taught in other grades. Teachers often read standards for their assigned grade levels and subjects without glancing at the standards and related units for grades flanking their own. It would behoove teachers to know what is taught before and after theirs—and even in additional grades—so they can plan appropriate instruction and avoid needless repetition. Certainly, students can benefit from frequent exposure to material for reinforcement, but if students are repeatedly presented with the same facts, skills, resources, and assessments, teachers are not serving them well. Creating a CYO that is in the students' best interest means that teachers have read other CYOs or standards in different grades and are aware of what other grade-level teachers are teaching. In this way, teachers can create their grade-level curricular maps and include references for making connections among concepts, introducing or reinforcing key skills in a thoughtful manner, scaffolding learning, and so forth.

Serve as a Marketing and Communications Tool

The CYO can be a useful tool to share with parents who are interested in what will be covered in a school year. Some teachers make the entire document available at back-to-school night; others share only the pacing of representative topics of the document. Some principals have the CYOs on hand for those community members interested in seeing it, or invite a key individual to present the CYO—or excerpts of it—at school board meetings. Sharing the entire CYO or excerpts with vested members of the school community can serve to illustrate teachers' professionalism. Teachers do not sing their own praises enough, and sharing CYOs is a vehicle to market the fine work that teachers do.

THE IMPORTANCE OF TEACHER SUPPORT

Collaborating with teachers to create Curriculum Year Overviews is usually part of the overarching goals of the school or district. The CYO should then be substantially supported by designing or identifying existing comprehensive curriculum plus instructional support, as needed. When the Curriculum Year Overview is created and amply supported by necessary curriculum plus instruction, teachers are equipped to thoroughly teach to the document so they can effectively serve students. This additional support is crucial and essentially a natural outgrowth of this document, because a CYO is definitely not a project done in isolation. The following scenarios can clarify my point:

1. *Wanted: Curriculum Resources.* As teachers convene to create a CYO, they examine grade-level content standards and carefully discuss their professional experiences with each applicable standard. In doing so, they often realize that they do not have the resources and materials to teach to a particular standard. It might be because it is a fairly new state or district standard, so the teachers do not have curriculum available. They are then tempted to write down only selected standards on the CYO, because they know they do not have the materials and resources to teach all the necessary standards. If administrators make it clear that teachers will have the necessary resources in time and money to obtain curriculum, materials, and even professional development to fully address each standard, they might be less hesitant to include all essential standards in the CYO.

2. *You Mean It Is Not My Standard?* As teachers review each standard for their grade and subject, they sometimes realize that a unit they have enjoyed teaching and perfecting for years does not necessarily fall under their jurisdiction. They discuss the hesitancy of offering their existing lessons and materials to the grade in which the standard is assigned. One reason for the reluctance is that they would then have to fill the time they spent teaching this unit with something else, and they lack resources and materials for an alternate unit of instruction. Another barrier to letting go of the unit is that teachers who have taught this content for years have invested a lot of time developing lessons and spending money for materials and resources. If, however, administrators make it clear that teachers will be granted the resources to obtain curriculum for a standard assigned to their grade and possibly release time or a stipend to develop a unit and gather additional materials, they might be willing to offer their existing lessons or unit to the grade for which the standard is designated.

3. *I Need to Go Back to School.* To expand on the aforementioned point, when teachers work on a CYO, they realize that some units of instruction they teach are not within their comfort level of expertise for a variety of reasons. I urge you to create an atmosphere that is inviting and comfortable enough for educators to express their concerns about teaching particular standards. Why? Because stating their feelings of inadequacy in certain areas paves the way for making a professional development plan in specific content areas for teachers who need it. The teacher who is uncomfortable teaching grammar can enroll in a class at a local community college, or someone needing assistance with a particular science concept can take an online course. It is critical that teachers receive the training necessary to teach effectively. Admitting what areas need improvement is a significant step toward obtaining the necessary support.

4. *We Need to Talk.* As a group of teachers work on a CYO, it is natural that they ask the question: "What should students come to my grade level knowing?" Equally important is the question: "What should we expect our students to know in preparation for the next grade?" Standards serve as a guide, but often they are not specific enough. A CYO opens the door for teachers to discuss answers to questions about what students should know when they leave and enter a grade. Articulation is a resounding theme as teachers work on the mapping document. In Chapter 3 are examples of projects that were by-products of a CYO that I have worked on with teachers for the express purpose of articulating and extending the information in the standards document for multiple grades.

Teachers will be more likely to develop a realistic and meaningful CYO if it is sufficiently supported. Therefore, administrators or other decision makers might consider appropriate budgeting and planning for one or more of the following. The end result would service students optimally, since the CYO sets the stage for more professional support for teachers so they can expand their expertise.

- Plan professional development days for the school or district.
- Arrange for district or school personnel or outside consultants.
- Provide curriculum resources and materials.
- Allow for release time to develop units of instruction, for conferences to build expertise in an area, to shadow colleagues, and so on.

POSSIBLE SITUATIONS

I have been fortunate to work with dedicated teaching professionals who take their work seriously and who consistently wish to hone their craft. In fact, this book could not have been written without the input from these creative, hard-working teachers. I would like to share some of my observations in working with them to assist you in your journey through the CYO process:

What if some teachers on a grade-level team do not want to help create a Curriculum Year Overview? I have learned along the way that it is essential to garner teachers' support and willingness to create a CYO prior to sitting around the table. But the reality is that this just may not happen. Sometimes, for a variety of reasons, not all grade-level team members are inclined to participate. A teacher about to retire may not be interested in devoting time to the project, a personality clash may exist among colleagues, a teacher may be on maternity leave or have other district or school commitments, and so on. If some are not interested, not all teachers in a particular grade level need to be involved in the process to create the CYO. For example, I have found that maybe two teachers out of a grade-level team of five decide they want to participate. Once it is complete and ready for piloting, others will hopefully see the value. They might ask for a copy or ask to be part of the review process and help with revision at a future date. Furthermore, those who are enthused about entering into this process might be hampered when sitting with colleagues who are less motivated and disenfranchised. Getting the best work from people is challenging when negative energy pervades the room. In addition to the buy-in factor, writing with this smaller group can be a more effective and efficient use of time. That said, administrators might feel compelled to involve all team members, including those who are uninterested. In this case, maybe a compromise would work, in which the first session includes everyone so all ideas are voiced, and subsequent meetings involve a smaller group of those most invested in the process.

What if teachers in a grade level do not satisfy standards in the same way? Some teachers who teach the same grade choose to plan together and teach the identical curriculum. In other schools or grades within a school, teachers approach standards differently based on their teaching styles and interests, but satisfy standards equally well. For example, one writing standard for seventh grade specifies that students produce a formal response to literature essay, at a minimum of 500 to 700 words. One teacher might assign students a collection of short stories, while another might expect students to respond to Jack London's novella *To Build a Fire*, and a third teacher might have students read a lengthy novel. Since there are a variety of ways teachers can satisfy standards, they can either find some common ground to include in the CYO or work separately to create different curriculum maps reflecting the practices of each teacher or group of teachers.

Are teachers usually familiar with standards for the grade they teach? In Chapter 2, you will find a detailed process for creating a CYO document. Near the beginning of producing it, you will allow time for teachers to peruse all the grade-level standards carefully so everyone is familiar with them, because you will likely be working with a diverse group of teachers with varying experience. Typically, teachers are not well versed in *all* the standards in a given grade level. This can happen because some standards are new to a grade level, teachers might be experienced but have been reassigned to a different grade level, teachers are inexperienced or new to the profession, or teachers simply have not taken the time to view them all because it was not made a priority. Even the most experienced teachers will need to study standards as you use them to assist with identifying skills, concepts, guiding questions, and so forth. The CYO is analogous to the fundamental framework for any balanced meal. Without teachers fully aware of what standards they are to teach, the meal is imbalanced; hence, the menu is incomplete and proper nutrition is compromised.

Can standards be reassigned to a different grade? I think it can work to reassign some standards to different grade levels within a school site, as long as they are developmentally appropriate for students and students graduate from that school exposed to all standards. For example in one school, teachers in sixth and seventh grades rearranged and regrouped the social studies and history standards so that students study geographical regions (e.g., Europe, Asia) together instead of time periods (e.g., Middle Ages, Renaissance). At the end of their time spent at this school, all students in sixth and seventh grades will still benefit from all social studies and history standards. I have seen this accomplished with science content standards, too. The decision to reassign standards to different grades is not something that a grade-level group can determine on its own, of course. It might not be a realistic option in some schools or districts because of standards mandates or because there is too much student mobility. But if this topic is broached during discussion, you might recommend that teachers approach their administrators and suggest designating a committee to discuss the viability of such an arrangement, examine all sides of the issue, and determine the process of engendering support and gaining approval.

Is this standard already being taught? One scenario I have encountered is teachers reading a standard and commenting, "Teachers address this standard in a different grade, but it is assigned to *our* grade level to teach." In this instance, I suggest that teachers meet with the other grade level to determine how much of the standard is met and how it is approached. It could be that another teacher is providing a cursory introduction, in which case teachers can thank their colleague in a prior grade for properly launching the unit that has served to prepare students for continued study. Or it might be that a teacher of a subsequent grade provides more in-depth instruction that further enhances the concept emanating from a standard. So teachers should speak with their colleagues to determine the end value for students. Have them focus the discussion on *how* the standard and its accompanying facts, concepts, and so on are specifically addressed to ensure that there is some variance and opportunity for learning growth. There might be value in teaching both units, because each lends itself to something meaningful for students at various levels of complexity, or it might be determined that one grade addresses the standard just fine and relegate the teaching to that grade level. Be cautious, though, to refer to the district's policy on the flexibility of switching standards to other grades to prime you for this discussion. Remember that one major purpose of creating a CYO is to document curriculum taught from one grade to the next, so teachers are cognizant of such articulation and can plan appropriately. We are not planning each menu item in isolation. The offerings need to complement one another for an overall well-rounded menu. You can suggest that participants undertake the project explained in Chapter 3, which focuses on articulation from grade to grade in very specific terms. In doing so, the issue of who teaches what and to what extent can be addressed formally.

SOME FINAL THOUGHTS

As you embark upon this project, know that it is hard work but realize it is an intensely rewarding project for teachers and for you as facilitator. Each time I work with teachers to create a CYO, they are amazed at the finished project that they will pilot. They are energized to begin planning and teaching with the new document in hand. The process of developing a CYO provides teachers a collaborative opportunity to discuss teaching approaches, analyze the value of teaching or not teaching certain units of study, examine and discuss philosophical similarities and differences, and share best practices. Most important, it allows teachers to think about, record, and implement different approaches to teaching a unit as they incorporate what they learn about skills, concepts, assessments, and guiding questions. In short, the work that transpires during the CYO process elevates teachers' level of professionalism. Learning something new is rewarding at any age.

2

The Process

This chapter explains the in-depth, step-by-step process for creating a Curriculum Year Overview. When the CYO is complete and ready for piloting, it will include:

- *Year-at-a-Glance:* The first two to four pages of the CYO provide a *cursory* glance of what the details of each unit include—representative topics, units of study, resources, and so on. See Figures 2.1 (second grade), 2.2 (fifth grade), and 2.3 (eighth grade) for examples.

- *Month-by-Month or Unit-by-Unit:* This is the comprehensive document that details an outline for each unit and serves as the basis for the CYO. It follows the "year-at-a-glance" pages. See these examples: Figures 2.4 (primary/"appreciation today and long ago"), Figure 2.5 (elementary/ "data/probability"), Figure 2.6 (upper elementary/"responding to literature"), Figure 2.7 (middle/"personal expression"), and Figure 2.8 (high school/ "societal injustice"). Mid-continent Research for Education and Learning (McREL) standards are included in all tables throughout the book. Pages 62 and 68 provide more information about McREL.

Whether or not a unit is interdisciplinary or single-subject, the following components are included and represent the format:

- Theme or unit topic
- Timing
- Unit guiding questions
- Standards
- Skills
- Assessments
- Resources

In this chapter, you will learn how to lead participants in creating their CYOs. "The Steps in the Process" chart (see page 13) details each step needed to facilitate a group. There are various options for the method you choose to record data for your curriculum map. You may create yours in Microsoft Word (table format) or Excel; you might use a computer mapping software program; or you might begin with Microsoft Word or Excel, and then hire a curriculum mapping software company to input your data and extend the capabilities of your CYO. See Chapter 5 for more detailed information about using curriculum mapping software programs.

TIMING

To create a typed and formatted CYO for the school year (approximately nine months of teaching) will probably take five days for self-contained classroom educators who teach about four subjects. For teachers of one or two subjects, the timing might be three to four full days. However, do not assume that because you are creating a curriculum map that represents fewer content areas, it will take fewer days. It might be that teachers who teach one or two subject areas choose to include more in their documents than teachers who work in self-contained classrooms. For example, language arts teachers might want to include monthly writing prompts along with the assessments for scoring these prompts. Similarly, math teachers may want to include monthly math prompts or problems of the week with their assessments. Although a typical CYO does not include these pieces, be mindful that this document is for teachers, and if it helps them to include routine milestones, make that option available.

These timing approximations are based on full release days or full days in the summer. Some teachers might even wish to work on Saturdays. If the teachers do not have these options available, then you will need to alter your timetable if you have a series of after-school sessions or half days spread throughout the summer or school year. Also, working online can expedite the process, so consider this along with face-to-face interactions. As you carefully review the step-by-step process in this chapter and take into consideration the time available to meet with teachers, teaching assignments, personalities, and so on, you can fashion a workable timetable that is right for you and your team.

Once you read through the entire chapter to understand each step, complete the Process Steps and Timetable Form (Figure 2.9) to organize the meetings. Do not feel that the meetings must occur in rapid succession. In fact, it is best to allow time in between to prepare for the next meeting and let everyone digest what has transpired.

Chart 2.1   The Steps in the Process

1. Making arrangements

2. Setting the stage

3. Reviewing content standards

4. Sketching the Year-at-a-Glance

5. Beginning the Curriculum Year Overview monthly units

6. Discussing standards not addressed

7. Developing unit guiding questions

8. Identifying skills and accompanying assessments

9. Listing resources

10. Identifying ongoing instruction or projects

11. Articulating across grade levels

12. Piloting and revising the document

Copyright © 2007 by Corwin Press. All rights reserved. Reprinted from *Curriculum Mapping: A Step-by-Step Guide for Creating Curriculum Year Overviews,* by Kathy Tuchman Glass. Thousand Oaks, CA: Corwin Press, www.corwinpress.com. Reproduction authorized only for the local school site or nonprofit organization that has purchased this book.

Figure 2.1   Second-Grade Year-at-a-Glance

Second-Grade Year-at-a-Glance

	FRIENDSHIP September/October	FAIRY TALES November/December	HEROES January/February	BEATRIX POTTER March	ALL ABOUT ME End of March – Mid-April	POETRY End of April – Mid-May	NOBODY'S PERFECT Mid-May – June
Social Studies	Geography and land use		Influential individuals	Basic economic concepts	Timeline of important life events	Family ancestry	Laws and basic government
Writing Types	Friendly letter	• Response to literature • Narrative	• Friendly letter (hero) • Biography	• Friendly letter (characters) • Narrative	Autobiography	• Poetry • Narrative	Narrative
Writing Prompts	• "Summer Story" • "Friendship"	Response to literature: "Rumpelstiltskin"	• "Magical" • "Power" • "Hero"	x	x	"Letter writing prompt"	x
Core Literature	Various stories from Houghton Mifflin and Scholastic texts	Various fairy tales from several sources	Various biography selections	Various Beatrix Potter books	*Miss Rumphius* by Barbara Cooney	Various poetry selections and family-related books	Various stories featuring prominent characters
Grammar/Conventions	• Capitalization • Verbs • Adjectives • Punctuation	• Pronouns • Sentence structure • Punctuation	• Punctuation • Nouns • Commas	• Grammar • Word usage	Vocabulary	Reference and information skills	Quotation marks
Science	Pebbles, sand, silt	Three types of matter: liquid, solid, gas	Weather	Living and nonliving		Dinosaurs	
Math	• Addition and subtraction facts to 20 • Place value	• Money • Two-digit addition and subtraction • Time • Interpreting and using data • Measurement	• Measurement • Geometry • Fractions • Probability	• Numbers to 1,000 • Add and subtract three-digit numbers		Multiplication and division	
Field Trips	Play: *Alexander and the Terrible, Horrible, No Good, Very Bad Day*	Play: *The Best Christmas Pageant Ever*	• Play: *The Ugly Duckling* • Firehouse	Phipps Ranch or Shaw's Candy	x	Hidden Villa	x
Ongoing Programs	Daily oral language	Daily oral geography		Spelling program	Reading groups	Handwriting program	

Copyright © 2007 by Corwin Press. All rights reserved. Reprinted from *Curriculum Mapping: A Step-by-Step Guide for Creating Curriculum Year Overviews*, by Kathy Tuchman Glass. Thousand Oaks, CA: Corwin Press, www.corwinpress.com. Reproduction authorized only for the local school site or nonprofit organization that has purchased this book.

Figure 2.2   Fifth-Grade Year-at-a-Glance

Fifth-Grade Year-at-a-Glance

	Social Studies	Literature	Writing	Presentations	Six Traits	Math	Science
September	Native Americans	*Castle in the Attic* by E. Winthrop	Narrative (short story)	*Time for Kids* all year long	Introduction of all six traits of writing	• Place value • Multiplication • Estimation • Division	Solar system
October	• Exploration • Cooperation/ conflict with Native Americans and new settlers	• *Castle in the Attic* (cont'd.) • Shakespeare bio • *Signatures/Coast to Coast*		Present short story			
November	Colonies	• *Indian in the Cupboard* by L.R. Banks • Shakespeare play	Response to literature	Present Colonial character role	• Ideas and content • Organization • Conventions	Fractions	Water
December	• Causes of the American Revolution • American Revolution	• *Indian in the Cupboard* (cont'd.) • Shakespeare play • *Signatures/Coast to Coast*		Present response to literature			Weather
January	Articles of Confederation	*The Black Stallion* by W. Farley				Measurement	
February	U.S. from 1789 to 1850/westward expansion	• *The Black Stallion* (cont'd.) • Shakespeare play • *Signatures/Coast to Coast*	Persuasive paper	Present persuasive paper	• Sentence fluency • Voice • Word choice • Conventions	Statistics and probability	Matter

(Continued)

15

Figure 2.2 (Continued)

	Social Studies	Literature	Writing	Presentations	Math	Science
March	Immigration from Europe between 1789 and 1850	*Bridge to Terabithia* by K. Patterson		*Time for Kids* (cont'd.)	Geometry	Plant systems
April	Geography/ physical and political	• *Bridge to Terabithia* (cont'd.) • *Signatures/ Coast to Coast*	Research report	Present research paper	• Decimals • Percentages	Animal systems
May	Statehood/ states and capitals	*Sign of the Beaver* by E.G. Speare		*Time for Kids* (cont'd.)	Algebra	• Human systems • Family life
June		• *Sign of the Beaver* (cont'd.) • *Signatures/Coast to Coast*	Poetry			Family life (cont'd.)

Copyright © 2007 by Corwin Press. All rights reserved. Reprinted from *Curriculum Mapping: A Step-by-Step Guide for Creating Curriculum Year Overviews*, by Kathy Tuchman Glass. Thousand Oaks, CA: Corwin Press, www.corwinpress.com. Reproduction authorized only for the local school site or nonprofit organization that has purchased this book.

Figure 2.3 Eighth-Grade Year-at-a-Glance

Eighth-Grade Year-at-a-Glance

	Social Studies	Literature	Writing/Presentation	Conventions	Science
September	CHANGE/CONTINUITY • Colonial America • Great Awakening • Causes of the Revolution • Declaration of Independence • American Revolution	Short stories (fiction): • "A Children's Story" • "Broken Chain" • "The Landlady" • "Mrs. Flowers" • "Lottery" • "The Tell-Tale Heart" • "The Circuit"	• Short stories • Response to literature [Students recite a section of the Declaration of Independence]	• Sentence structures (types): compound, complex, etc. • Sentence openings • Grammar • Punctuation	MOTION • Velocity • Average speed • Interpreting graphs
October	GOVERNMENT SYSTEMS • Documents • U.S. Constitution • Articles of Confederation • Major debates and political philosophy	*Johnny Tremain* by Esther Forbes	• Short stories • Response to literature [Students recite the Preamble]	• Capitalization • Spelling	FORCES • Balanced and unbalanced forces • Gravity
November	GOVERNMENT SYSTEMS • State constitutions • Ordinances • Political parties • Domestic resistance • Political process • Free press	• "Harrison Bergeron" • *The Giver* by Lois Lowry	• Response to literature • Persuasive [Amendment project presented to the class]	• Parallelism • Grammar • Punctuation • Capitalization • Spelling	STRUCTURE OF MATTER • Structure of atoms • Compounds • Electrons
December	CULTURES • People of the new nation • Capitalism FOREIGN POLICY • War of 1812 • Monroe Doctrine • Native American treaties		• Persuasive (cont'd.) • Response to literature [Proposed bill presented to the class]		STRUCTURE OF MATTER (cont'd.) • Solids, liquids, gasses

(Continued)

Figure 2.3 (Continued)

	Social Studies	Literature	Writing/[Presentation]	Conventions	Science
January	REFORM	Poetry	• Poetry • Response to literature [Poem presented to class]	• Apposition • Grammar • Punctuation • Capitalization • Spelling	• Periodic table • Isotopes CHEMICAL REACTIONS
February	STRIVING FOR INDEPENDENCE • Abolitionists • Northwest Ordinance • Compromise of 1850 • States' Rights Doctrine • Missouri Compromise • Free Blacks	*Flowers for Algernon* by Daniel Keyes	• Research report • Response to literature	• Grammar • Punctuation • Capitalization • Spelling • Bibliography	
March	CONFLICT/ COOPERATION • Causes of the Civil War • Civil War	Civil War literature circles (differentiated list): • *With Every Drop of Blood* by James and Christopher Collier • *Killer Angels* by Michael Shaara • *Amelia's War* by Ann Rinaldi • *No Man's Land* by Susan Bartoletti • *Bull Run* by Paul Fleischman • *Abraham's Battle* by Sara Banks			CHEMISTRY OF LIVING THINGS • Carbon and its role • Living organisms
April		• *Soldier's Heart* by Gary Paulsen • *Voices of the Civil War* by Richard Wheeler • *A Photobiography of Abraham Lincoln* by Russell Freedman	• Documents related to career development • Response to literature	• Grammar • Punctuation • Capitalization • Spelling	• DENSITY • BUOYANCY
May/June	ECONOMIC TRANSFORMATION	*The Pearl* by John Steinbeck		Review of all skills	EARTH IN THE SOLAR SYSTEM • Galaxies • Stars • Solar system

Copyright © 2007 by Corwin Press. All rights reserved. Reprinted from *Curriculum Mapping: A Step-by-Step Guide for Creating Curriculum Year Overviews*, by Kathy Tuchman Glass. Thousand Oaks, CA: Corwin Press. www.corwinpress.com. Reproduction authorized only for the local school site or nonprofit organization that has purchased this book.

Figure 2.4   Unit: Thanksgiving—Appreciation Today and Long Ago

Thanksgiving: Appreciation Today and Long Ago

Timing: November—Grades: Primary
Unit Guiding Questions: 1. Why is Thanksgiving a holiday? **2.** Why are you thankful? **3.** How can you show your appreciation and thanks to others? **4.** How was life long ago different and the same from life today? **5.** How have Native Americans contributed to society?

McREL STANDARDS	SKILLS/ACTIVITIES	ASSESSMENTS	RESOURCES
Social Studies • Understands the reasons that Americans celebrate certain national holidays • Knows the cultural similarities and differences in the clothes, homes, food, communication, and cultural traditions between families now and in the past • Understands the daily life of a colonial community • Understands the daily life and values of early Native American cultures • Understands through legends, myths the origins and culture of early Native Americans **Reading** • Uses mental images based on pictures and print to aid in comprehension of text • Uses reading skills and strategies to understand a variety of informational texts and literary works (e.g., myths and folktales) • Understands the main idea and supporting details of simple expository information • Summarizes information found in texts (e.g., retells in own words) • Relates new information to prior knowledge and experience **Writing** • Uses writing to describe persons and places • Writes for different purposes (e.g., to inform) • Uses conventions of print in writing (e.g., forms letters in print, uses upper- and lowercase letters, spaces, words and sentences) • Uses complete sentences in written compositions • Uses conventions of spelling in written compositions (e.g., spells high-frequency words, uses letter-sound relationships) • Uses conventions of capitalization in written compositions (e.g., first and last names, first words of a sentence) • Uses conventions of punctuation in written compositions (e.g., uses periods after declarative sentences) **Math** • Selects and uses appropriate tools for measurement situations • Understands and applies basic and advanced properties of the concept of measurement **Art** • Uses a variety of basic art materials to create works of art and express ideas and feelings	• Retell the historical origin for celebrating Thanksgiving • Brainstorm reasons for being thankful • Compare and contrast various aspects of daily and family life today versus long ago: clothing, home, food, communication, transportation, traditions • Identify similarities and differences among various Native American creation myths and folktales • List contributions Native Americans have made • Comprehend and summarize what is read • Write and draw main idea of what is learned • Identify and express in writing personal feelings • Use appropriate measuring tools • Listen and follow instructions to make butter, jam, and cornbread muffins • Weave placemats • Trace hands • Use scissors	• Venn diagram of life then and now • Story maps of characters, setting, problem/solution in myths and folktales • Observation of classroom participation and discussion Through interactive writing, teacher support, and individually, students produce the following writing: • Book with pictures and words that detail what Native Americans have brought to our way of life (e.g., farming methods, food, etc.) • "I Am Thankful" class book explaining what each student is thankful for • Written response to one prompt: "If I were a Pilgrim . . ." or "If I could say something to Squanto, I would say . . ." • Butter, jam, and cornbread muffins • Classroom observations • Placemats • Hand turkeys • Collage	• Various historical fiction and nonfiction for the study of Thanksgiving, Native Americans, Pilgrims • Various creation myths and folktales • Journals • Various graphic organizers • Cooking utensils and supplies • Cookbook • Art supplies • Weaving materials • Pictures of turkeys

NOTE: Standards and Benchmarks are used and/or adapted by permission of McREL. Copyright © 2004, McREL.

Reprinted from *Curriculum Mapping: A Step-by-Step Guide for Creating Curriculum Year Overviews* by Kathy Tuchman Glass. Thousand Oaks, CA: Corwin Press, www.corwinpress.com. Reproduction authorized only for the local school site or nonprofit organization that has purchased this book.

Figure 2.5   Unit: Data/Probability

UNIT: Data/Probability—TIMING: September				
Guiding Questions: 1. How do we make, read and interpret graphs to gather information? **2.** How do we make predictions using data? **3.** How do people use graphs in the world? **4.** How might I use graphs in my life?			
McREL STANDARDS	**SKILLS**	**ASSESSMENTS**	**RESOURCES**
• Understands that data represent specific pieces of information about real-world objects or activities • Organizes and displays data in simple bar graphs, pie charts, and line graphs • Reads and interprets simple bar graphs, pie charts, and line graphs • Understands that data come in many different forms and that collecting, organizing, and displaying data can be done in many ways • Recognizes events that are sure to happen, events that are sure not to happen, and events that may or may not happen (e.g., in terms of "certain," "uncertain," "likely," "unlikely") • Uses basic sample spaces to describe and predict events	• Collect data in the form of a survey and record results • Read and interpret data in a line plot, pictograph, bar graph, and table • Make a line plot, pictograph, bar graph, and table • Use ordered pairs to identify the points in an ordered plane • Use information from a line plot, bar graph, table, or pictograph to solve problems • Experiment with probability and record the data • Use experimental results to make predictions and/or decide if an event is certain, likely, unlikely, or impossible	• Tables, bar graphs, pictographs, and line plots using information gathered from class surveys (i.e., birthdays, pets, sports, family members) • Teacher observation and classroom participation • Worksheet pages (as appropriate) • Oral and written responses to problems • Recorded results from probability games using manipulatives (i.e., dice, spinners, tiles) • Group work and class observation • Quizzes and test	• *Houghton Mifflin Mathematics,* Chapter 10 (copyright 2002) • Graph paper • Math manipulatives (i.e., spinners, tiles, dice) • Overhead transparencies from supplemental textbook materials • Teacher display of charts, graphs, newspapers • Various teacher resources • Software: "Kidspiration" to make graphs

NOTE: Standards and Benchmarks are used and/or adapted by permission of McREL. Copyright © 2004, McREL.

Reprinted from *Curriculum Mapping: A Step-by-Step Guide for Creating Curriculum Year Overviews* by Kathy Tuchman Glass. Thousand Oaks, CA: Corwin Press, www.corwinpress.com. Reproduction authorized only for the local school site or nonprofit organization that has purchased this book.

Figure 2.6 Unit: Responding to Literature

UNIT: Responding to Literature—TIMING: November		

Response to Literature Unit Guiding Questions: 1. How do readers respond thoughtfully to literature? **2.** Why is it important to respond to literature with insights and interpretations? **3.** How is a response to literature paper organized and written?

SKILLS	ASSESSMENTS	RESOURCES
Response to Literature Writing • Summarizes main ideas and significant details • Relates own ideas to supporting details • Advances judgment • Supports judgments with references to text, other works, other authors, and personal knowledge • Identifies audience/purpose • Uses the writing process • Uses proper grammar and conventions • Uses descriptive language • Indents and uses rules of paragraphing • Varies sentence structure **Reading** • Uses reading strategies: pause, reread, consult another source, draw upon background knowledge, ask for help • Uses context clues to decode unknown words • Defines elements of literature and identifies how they interrelate in reading selections (i.e., plot, setting, character, point of view, theme)	• Teacher observation • Classroom participation in whole-class and small-group discussions and activities • Oral and written response to literature • Journals • Formal written response to literature scored against genre-based rubric	• *Open Court* textbook and supplemental materials • *WriteTraits Student Traitbook* and *WriteTraits Teacher's Guide* (Great Source Education Group) • Thesaurus • Dictionary • Various literature

McREL STANDARDS	
Writing • Uses the general skills and strategies of the **writing process:** prewriting, drafting and revising, editing and publishing • **Evaluates** own and others' **writing** • Uses strategies to write for different **audiences** and for a variety of **purposes** • **Writes response to literature** • Uses **descriptive language** that clarifies and enhances ideas • Uses **paragraph** form in writing • Uses a variety of **sentence structures** in writing • Uses conventions of **spelling** in written composition • Uses conventions of **capitalization** and **punctuation** in written composition **Reading** • **Uses reading skills and strategies** to understand a variety of literature passages and texts	• Makes, confirms, and revises simple **predictions** about what will be found in the text • Understands the basic concept of **plot** • Understands elements of **character** development in literary works • Knows **themes** that recur across literary works • Makes **connections** between characters or simple events in a literary work and people or events In his or her own life **Listening and Speaking** • Contributes **to group discussions** • **Asks questions** in class • **Responds to questions and comments**

NOTE: Standards and Benchmarks are used and/or adapted by permission of McREL. Copyright © 2004, McREL.

Reprinted from *Curriculum Mapping: A Step-by-Step Guide for Creating Curriculum Year Overviews* by Kathy Tuchman Glass. Thousand Oaks, CA: Corwin Press, www.corwinpress.com. Reproduction authorized only for the local school site or nonprofit organization that has purchased this book.

Figure 2.7   Unit: Point of View—Personal Expression

UNIT: Point of View—Personal Expression—TIMING: September

Reading/Writing Guiding Questions: 1. How can people express who they are through words? **2.** How can others prompt responses in writers? **3.** How does figurative language make writing stronger? **4.** How can I express who I am through poetry?

SKILLS	ASSESSMENTS	RESOURCES
• Identify features of poetry • Define how tone is conveyed in poetry • Identify and analyze figurative language to determine the effect on the writing • Read and identify author's point of view and purpose for writing • Interpret the words of a writer through careful reading, understanding, and insight • Write poetry using poetic features to express self • Present poetry using inflection/modulation of voice, tempo, volume, enunciation, eye contact, posture	• Classroom discussion • Oral presentation • "I Am From" poem scored against a rubric • Outlines or notes • Student journals	• *Love That Dog* by Sharon Creech (read aloud) • "In a Neighborhood in Los Angeles" by Francisco X. Alarcon • "Ode to Mi Gato" by Gary Soto • "Hard on the Gas" by Janet Wong • Enid Lee, author and guest speaker

McREL STANDARDS

Writing
• Writes descriptive **poetry**
• Uses precise and **descriptive language** that clarifies and enhances ideas (e.g., establishes tone, uses figurative language, uses sensory images and comparisons)
• Uses content, style, and structure appropriate for specific **audiences** and **purposes**
• Uses the strategies of the **writing process:** prewriting, drafting and revising, editing and publishing
• **Evaluates** own and others' **writing**

Reading
• Uses **reading skills and strategies** to understand a variety of literary passages
• Understands the **use of language** in literary works to convey mood, images, and meaning (e.g., rhyme, voice, tone, sound, figurative language)

Listening and Speaking
• Makes **oral presentations** to the class
• Uses **verbal and nonverbal techniques** for oral presentations

NOTE: Standards and Benchmarks are used and/or adapted by permission of McREL. © Copyright c 2004, McREL.

Reprinted from *Curriculum Mapping: A Step-by-Step Guide for Creating Curriculum Year Overviews* by Kathy Tuchman Glass. Thousand Oaks, CA: Corwin Press, www.corwinpress.com. Reproduction authorized only for the local school site or nonprofit organization that has purchased this book.

Figure 2.8   Unit: Societal Injustice

UNIT: Societal Injustice—*The Crucible and McCarthyism*—TIMING: September

Guiding Questions: 1. How did Puritan society instill fear? **2.** How are individuals affected by society? **3.** Why might Proctor be called a tragic hero? **4.** How is human weakness shown in *The Crucible*? **5.** How do the themes and events in *The Crucible* parallel the McCarthy era? **6.** How do the themes of the play relate to modern social issues? **7.** How has the author's perspective shaped this play?

McREL STANDARDS:

Writing
- Uses the general skills and strategies of the writing process
- Uses the stylistic and rhetorical aspects of writing
- Uses grammatical and mechanical conventions in written compositions

Reading
- Uses the general skills and strategies of the reading process
- Uses reading skills and strategies to understand and interpret a variety of literary texts
- Uses reading skills and strategies to understand and interpret a variety of informational texts

Skills/Activities:
- Write a response to literature essay using the writing process steps: prewriting, drafting, revising, editing, publishing
- Organize the paper for a response-to-literature format; see "Assessment" for specifics of paper content and format
- Write a variety of sentence types (e.g., simple, compound, complex)
- Organize ideas to provide cohesion and balance in paper
- Divide paragraphs appropriately and include transitional words and phrases
- Write with an understanding of audience and purpose
- Employ appropriate reading strategies
- Extrapolate salient points from text

Assessment:
- Participation in class and small-group discussion
- Graphic organizers and notes
- Response to literature essay scored against rubric that:
  - Demonstrates a comprehensive grasp of the significant ideas of literary works;
  - Supports important ideas and viewpoints through accurate and detailed references to the text or to other works;
  - Demonstrates awareness of the author's use of stylistic devices and an appreciation of the effects created;
  - Identifies and assesses the impact of perceived ambiguities, nuances, and complexities within the text.

History
- Understands the role of McCarthyism in the early Cold War period (e.g., the rise of McCarthyism, the effect of McCarthyism on civil liberties, and McCarthy's fall from power; the connection between postwar Soviet espionage and internal security and loyalty programs under Truman and Eisenhower)

Skills:
- Create a timeline
- Write a well-balanced, accurate, and insightful essay using proper writing conventions and strategies of the writing process
- Employ appropriate reading skills and strategies
- Compare/contrast information on the same topic gleaned from many resources

Assessment:
- Annotated timeline about the rise of McCarthyism and McCarthy's fall from power
- Analytical essay about the effects of McCarthyism on civil liberties; scored against rubric

Resources: *The Crucible* by Arthur Miller; commentaries on *The Crucible;* social studies textbook; response to literature student and published samples; literature textbook as resource for response to literature writing; various secondary and primary resources for McCarthyism

NOTE: Standards and Benchmarks are used and/or adapted by permission of McREL. Copyright © 2004, McREL.

Reprinted from *Curriculum Mapping: A Step-by-Step Guide for Creating Curriculum Year Overviews* by Kathy Tuchman Glass. Thousand Oaks, CA: Corwin Press, www.corwinpress.com. Reproduction authorized only for the local school site or nonprofit organization that has purchased this book.

Figure 2.9   Process Steps and Timetable

The Steps in the Process	Date/Time of Session	Location
1. Making Arrangements		
2. Setting the Stage		
3. Reviewing Content Standards		
4. Sketching the "Year-at-a-Glance"		
5. Beginning the Curriculum Year Overview Monthly Units		
6. Discussing Standards Not Addressed		
7. Developing Unit Guiding Questions		
8. Identifying Skills and Accompanying Assessments		
9. Listing Resources		
10. Identifying Ongoing Instruction or Projects		
11. Articulating Across Grade Levels		
12. Piloting and Revising the Document		

Copyright © 2007 by Corwin Press. All rights reserved. Reprinted from *Curriculum Mapping: A Step-by-Step Guide for Creating Curriculum Year Overviews*, by Kathy Tuchman Glass. Thousand Oaks, CA: Corwin Press, www.corwinpress.com. Reproduction authorized only for the local school site or nonprofit organization that has purchased this book.

THE STEPS IN THE PROCESS

STEP ONE: Making Arrangements

It is imperative that you choreograph and plan for each meeting. What follows is the detailed preparation for the first meeting so that you can successfully launch this project.

1. Select a ***location*** and choose a ***date*** for your first meeting. I suggest you meet in a quiet place where interruptions can be kept to a minimum. If your group meets on a staff development day or after school, a classroom is optimal, because all the materials and resources are at hand, and the educational ambience is an added benefit. If you meet when school is in session, I suggest an off-site location free of interruptions from administration, substitutes, students, phone calls, and so on. I invite most clients to my home, so consider meeting at someone's home or at another location that is relatively serene so you can get a lot accomplished.

2. I emphasize ***dressing comfortably***, but this is a personal decision. I work best when wearing nonbinding clothes, because I'm sure to eat more than my share of tasty treats during the creation process! If I feel hampered in any way, my creativity is stifled. But truly, you may not be a junk-food junkie like me, so ignore this piece of advice if it is non-applicable.

3. After it has been established that this project will be undertaken, I suggest sending an ***e-mail*** or ***memo*** to your group alerting them of the date, place, and time of your first meeting. Facilitators can use the letter in Figure 2.10 and just fill in the appropriate blanks, add a signature, and attach any necessary directions, or use it as a guide to create a similar letter.

4. Continuing with the metaphor for a CYO stated earlier, when chefs begin cooking, they lay out necessary utensils and appliances. I recommend the same for teachers during this project of curriculum overview planning. When you work with them to plan the teaching year, it is critical that they ***bring materials and resources*** to the first and subsequent meetings. As you work together on this project, some of these tools and resources—like a chef's spatula and food processor—will be incorporated into the final creation. In addition, participants can identify what materials and resources they do not currently have but wish to obtain.

- The letter in Figure 2.10 includes a list of materials, along with other logistical information for the first meeting. Read it to determine if the list of suggested materials is appropriate for this first gathering.
- Other suggestions: (1) You might rewrite the letter in Figure 2.10 and delete some items for your first meeting, or (2) rewrite the letter in Figure 2.10 to include some items from Figure 2.11 ("Materials"), which provides an extensive list of suggested items. How much time you have with your group will help determine what materials to bring, or (3) you might write a cover letter, attach

Figure 2.11, and send this prior to each meeting. Be mindful that the note at the top of the list in Figure 2.11 instructs teachers to bring only those items you have checked. They might be overwhelmed to think that they would have to lug everything listed to each meeting.

- Note that not all teachers will have everything listed, but ask them to bring what they do have. They will naturally want to share their materials and resources.

5. You will need a **computer or laptop** to record the input from participants as you lead them through the mapping process. The finished document is word-processed, so you may want to begin keyboarding from the start.

6. As the facilitator, you might **bring copies of the pertinent content standards** for the participants. I typically do this, because teachers bring so many materials and resources to the meeting that furnishing the standards for them is a big help. For accessing your state's content standards, here are two Web sites that list links to every state's standards:

- National Center on Educational Outcomes
  - http://education.umn.edu/nceo/TopicAreas/Standards/States Standards.htm
- Education World
  - http://www.education-world.com/standards/state/index.shtml

If you choose to bring the standards, delete this item from the "Materials" list (Figure 2.11) or simply do not check it when notifying participants what to bring. It is on the list in case participants already have their content standards. When facilitating groups in creating a CYO, I find it particularly helpful to **have the standards for all subject areas and grades loaded into my laptop.** So, have content standards ready on your laptop, as well as content standards in hard copy to give to participants if needed. Make sure that you have downloaded onto your computer the standards for all grades, because invariably other grade-level standards will come up in the conversation. If the school in which you are working has an Internet connection, you can conceivably access these standards online at the meeting. But it is more reliable to have the standards already downloaded and in an easily accessible Microsoft Word file.

7. As facilitator, you might want to bring **this book** so you can access sections or specific pages that you want to share with others. Or you may want to purchase books for the group.

Figure 2.10 Letter to Teachers

Dear Teachers,

On _____ (date), I will work with you on a curriculum mapping project that will allow you to plot and identify your entire grade-level curriculum standards, key concepts and skills, assessments, and resources for the school year. To make our time together worthwhile, please come to our first session armed with the following materials:

• Bring any sheet you have created that contains planning for the year. This could be in your lesson plan book or a separate sheet that briefly or not so briefly lists what you might plan to teach for a particular unit and/or the entire school year.

• Bring any textbooks kids have access to for ALL the subject areas you teach—math, literature, grammar resource books, etc.

• For each unit you teach, you probably have additional books that you use beyond the textbook. Please bring a list of these books.

• If you teach language arts, bring a list of novels and other literature along with the authors and genres of the books (e.g., contemporary realistic fiction, historical fiction, autobiography, etc.).

• Bring any assessments that you use with kids for specific units of instruction.

• Bring a school calendar listing vacation days, assemblies, team meetings, and other school-related events and days off for students.

We will meet _____ (location) at _____ until _____ (time). I look forward to seeing the fruits of our labor as this document will help guide you throughout the year and allow you to look carefully at your curricular program. This project is ongoing, so together we can agree on subsequent dates and times at this meeting. Please bring your calendar so we can plan these future meetings.

Thanks for all you do!

Best regards,

Copyright © 2007 by Corwin Press. All rights reserved. Reprinted from *Curriculum Mapping: A Step-by-Step Guide for Creating Curriculum Year Overviews,* by Kathy Tuchman Glass. Thousand Oaks, CA: Corwin Press, www. corwinpress. com. Reproduction authorized only for the local school site or nonprofit organization that has purchased this book.

Figure 2.11 Materials

Materials

As we embark upon a project to create a Curriculum Year Overview that maps out your school year, come prepared with the materials that are checked and are available to you from the list below. It is expected that you may not have access to some of the line items listed. Again, you do not need to bring all materials to each meeting; only bring those items checked for the upcoming meeting.

☐ Bring whatever you have created that contains **PLANNING FOR THE YEAR**. This could be your lesson plan book or a separate sheet that briefly or not so briefly lists what you might plan to teach for a particular unit or the entire school year. It might even be a brief or comprehensive outline you inherited from a former teacher who taught the grade you do now.

☐ Bring a **JOB DESCRIPTION** from the school or district if one was ever created for your particular position.

☐ Bring a **SCHOOL CALENDAR** that details all the holidays, minimum days, staff development or other days students have off from school, plus the start and end dates for the school year.

☐ Bring the **STATE OR DISTRICT CONTENT STANDARDS** for all of the subjects you teach and wish to include in the Curriculum Year Overview. It is preferable that you make copies of the grade-level content standards so you can write, highlight, and doodle on them. You can go online and find your state's content standards to print out if they are what your school subscribes to; otherwise, get ahold of your district standards. It is also recommended that you find and bring standards for a cluster of grades surrounding your own so you can see expected standards in the grades before and after the ones you teach and even beyond. Even if your state or district standards are written in grade-level clusters, you might have to bring the next cluster if your grade is on the cusp. For example, if you teach sixth grade, bring the third- to fifth-grade cluster of standards and the sixth- to eighth-grade cluster. If a CYO has already been created for these other grades and includes standards, then just bring that. Invariably, you will refer to different grades' standards to see expectations.

☐ If your school or district has done work on **GUIDING QUESTIONS**, then bring these for the subject area you teach for any unit of instruction or for a discipline.

☐ Bring **TEXTBOOKS STUDENTS HAVE ACCESS** to for ALL the subject areas you teach—science, math, literature, grammar resource books, etc. Bring the teachers' editions. If there are several teachers' editions, bring the first two volumes or units to the first meeting. If your school is adopting a new textbook and the books are not yet in, find a copy of the textbook to use while creating this curriculum overview. Ask those on the textbook adoption committee if you can borrow a book, or call the publisher's representative to ask for a textbook in advance. Most likely, they will send you a sample copy free of charge.

☐ Bring any useful **ANCILLARY MATERIALS** that accompany the textbook and **TEACHER RESOURCES** that you have for your units of study. If you prefer, you can bring a list of titles and publishers for the resources since there will be many, I imagine. (A rolling cart might be a welcome treat right about now.)

☐ For each comprehensive unit of study, you probably assign a **CULMINATING ASSESSMENT** (i.e., culminating product, project, or assignment) that is meaningful and standards-based. Bring either the actual student assignment sheets or a list explaining these assessments from various units. As you create your document, you may want to alter the assessments, but bring what you have so you can review and discuss their effectiveness.

☐ If you teach language arts, bring a **LIST OF CORE LITERATURE BOOKS** along with the authors and genres of the books (e.g., contemporary realistic fiction, historical fiction, autobiography, etc.). If you have students engage in literature circles, bring a list of those books with authors, too. For primary teachers, decide which books you want to reference in your document and bring a list of those books and authors. Some reading selections might be listed in your literature textbook, so bring the anthology.

☐ Think about the **FORMAL ASSESSMENTS**. These include formal classroom assessments not linked to a particular unit, district and school assessments, plus state testing. You might want to reference these assessments in your document at the appropriate times throughout the year or ongoing. For example, you might issue a formal reading, writing, or math assessment in your classroom in September to gauge students' abilities and plan instruction accordingly.

Copyright © 2007 by Corwin Press. All rights reserved. Reprinted from *Curriculum Mapping: A Step-by-Step Guide for Creating Curriculum Year Overviews*, by Kathy Tuchman Glass. Thousand Oaks, CA: Corwin Press, www.corwinpress.com. Reproduction authorized only for the local school site or nonprofit organization that has purchased this book.

STEP TWO: Setting the Stage

The way you begin the first meeting sets the stage for your work with the participating teachers. Follow the recommendations below to assist you in effectively commencing the Curriculum Year Overview project.

1. Imagine sitting around a large table laden with teachers' **resources and materials**. A **laptop** might be booting up. **Pencils** are sharpened; **pads of paper** are available. I even put out **sticky pads**. The ambience should be conducive to the task at hand; **coffee and sodas** stand ready next to a plate of salty or sweet **snacks**. **Lunch** has been ordered in advance if this is a full-day meeting.

2. If you are working with a group of teachers who do not all know each other, allow time for **introductions**. Invite each person to say his or her name and give some background information. Even if some have met, take time for introductions so that everyone in the room is formally introduced. As the facilitator for a group of teachers, share your qualifications and how you got involved in this project.

3. Use the **metaphor of a chef** for a CYO and explain that you see the work of this curriculum map as the balanced meal that is the fundamental framework and first step. This will help set the stage for your work together.

- The CYO is the basic meal of a protein, starch, and vegetable that is the starting point for chefs as they build menus.
- The units referenced in the CYO represent specific menu items based on the balanced meals (e.g., steak as the protein, potato as the starch, asparagus as the vegetable).
- Articulation is reflective in the other menu items added, such as wine, appetizers, and desserts.
- All committed professionals evaluate and revise their work accordingly. A chef might add new menu items and delete others based on customer satisfaction or dissatisfaction and availability of ingredients. So is true of a teacher who revisits the CYO and makes changes and revisions based on a variety of factors.
- The specific comprehensive units including lesson details for execution, handouts, and so on are the recipes for the basic meal. This detail is not included in the CYO.

4. **Review the definition and purposes** for creating a CYO by highlighting information found in **Chapter 1**. Everyone in the room should be clear about the purposes for creating the document, which serves to map out their school year.

5. Be clear that the CYO should serve as a very **usable document** to chart the year, but that it should not include specific lessons. Remember that it is the **outline**—or menu offerings and not specific recipes. The comprehensive curriculum units are clearly referenced in the CYO, but they are housed separately in individual binders, hanging folders, or teachers' manuals. The group with whom you work will determine how extensive the outline will become.

6. Ask each teacher what he or she **hopes to accomplish** as a final product. Although each has an idea of the task at hand, you might probe them to determine what each expects out of your time together. Since teachers are at

different places in terms of teaching experience at a given grade level and teaching in general, this is an important discussion.

7. The participants you work with teach single subjects in one class period, core subjects (language arts/social studies) for a double- or three-period core, or multiple subjects in self-contained classrooms. Some will employ interdisciplinary teaching or themes to drive a unit, while others teach in a different manner. The configuration of the teaching assignments will drive the text of the Curriculum Year Overview, although the essential format will remain the same. Make sure you *know the teaching assignments of the teachers in your group* so that you are familiar with your clientele.

8. Direct everyone's attention to the *CYO samples in Chapter 4* that most closely resemble their teaching assignments—not the "Year-at-a Glance" pages, but the *monthly detailed unit outlines.* You will find examples of thematic units, core units (social studies and language arts), and single-subject units. One particular grade level might include core *and* single-subject (e.g., fifth grade) units. As facilitator, *be well versed in the samples* so you know in advance which ones you will show to the group and can reference pertinent samples easily. Show them the format for all pages: title, guiding questions, standards, skills, assessments, and resources. You want teachers to see these examples so they have an idea of what the finished product will be. Assure them that you will guide them to complete this project and even if it seems daunting, you will take them step by step through a process that makes it less cumbersome. And even when the document is finished, it will be piloted and revised, so it is essentially a work-in-progress. Step Twelve is specifically devoted to revision of the document.

STEP THREE: Reviewing Content Standards

I ask teachers to come to the meeting about standards without any preparation other than what they already know, so we can discuss content standards as a group. Invariably, as we peruse them together, they become enlightened about a standard and learn they have been teaching what they need not, are not teaching what they ought to, or are unclear about a particular standard. This is to be expected, so take the time to delve into answers to questions and further investigation. Create an atmosphere that encourages teachers to discuss and examine the standards in detail, so there is more awareness and willingness to teach to them. If there are standards that teachers feel are developmentally inappropriate, encourage them to initiate an open dialogue with administration, as mentioned in Chapter 1. If some standards are vaguely written—and this happens quite often—determine as a group how to interpret the standards in question so all teachers are working with the same definitions. In Step Seven, you will facilitate an exercise in which teachers craft guiding questions from standards. This will serve to translate these standards in a usable way to guide student learning. What follows is a recommended procedure for identifying targeted standards and any themes for specific units of study.

1. Participants *take out copies of the contents standards* for the appropriate grades and subjects they teach, along with a highlighter and pencil. As mentioned in Chapter 1, teachers can bring copies of standards they can write on, *or* you can furnish copies of standards for the group.

2. If teachers teach more than one subject, ***discuss which discipline they choose to start with and begin there.*** If they teach through interdisciplinary instruction, choose the subject area that might serve as the focus for a particular unit. For example, if students study the daily life and culture of Native Americans and then write Native American myths, begin with social studies standards and then later augment language arts standards with reading and writing creation myths.

3. Instruct participants to first ***read through the standards of the chosen content area silently.*** As they read, ask them to ***make notations*** for the following:

- *Group together any standards* that form the basis for a unit of study. If it is an interdisciplinary unit, also peruse the appropriate standards for other content areas now or later as your group determines.
- Alongside the standards, *write down a unit's theme name or concept* (e.g., "Patterns," "Conflicts," "Government systems") *and representative topic* (e.g., "Causes of the Revolution," "Rocks and minerals," "Geometry"). Copy and distribute Figure 2.12, which includes a list of various concepts participants can have on hand. These concepts were compiled from a variety of sources. Feel free to add other concepts and macroconcepts that you have found in your studies. Encourage teachers to frame their units for conceptual understanding by identifying the overarching concept of a unit of study tied to the representative topic (e.g., "How Plants Grow and Change: Sunflowers" or "Government Systems: The Constitution as Law of the Land"). This may take some time, but it is critical that teachers understand what the essential learning of a given unit entails instead of just listing a topic, such as "Electricity" or "Geography." Discussing the essence of a unit of study will lead to identifying its concept.
- *Indicate which month*(s) this unit of study is taught.
- If there are standards addressed as instruction for a *daily or weekly routine,* indicate the ongoing instruction and put an asterisk by these standards—for example, writing in a daily journal, conducting a calendar activity each morning, solving math problems of the week, or summarizing science content.
- If there are *standards that are not addressed,* highlight them for a later discussion with the group. (See Step Six.)

4. Once participants have made notations independently, begin a conversation around the table, in which ***teachers share their notes with one another.*** There might be differing views on which standards to group together, the name of a thematic unit, or the month a unit is taught. Lead teachers in arriving at a consensus. During this part of the process, a fruitful discussion ensues as teachers share what they have done and what they would do better next year. New teachers or those new to a particular grade, who may not necessarily have a lot to contribute, gain much from listening to colleagues. Another byproduct of this discussion is that teachers who highlighted standards that they do not meet can be enlightened by another teacher's use of them within a unit of study.

5. At the end of this exercise, your **_goal_** is for teachers to identify concepts and representative topics, the accompanying standards or group of standards, and the months when these units are taught. Also, delineate which standards are not addressed at all and those that are part of a daily or weekly routine.

STEP FOUR: Sketching the "Year-at-a-Glance"

After teachers have discussed their year in general by using standards as the vehicle for discussion, begin to draft the overarching year on a template called "Year-at-a-Glance." It is from the work of these few pages that the details of the Curriculum Year Overview are based.

1. In Step Two, "Setting the Stage," you showed teachers what the detailed units would entail by sharing samples from this book. Now **_show_** participants the **_"Year-at-a-Glance"_** samples (Figures 2.1, 2.2, and 2.3) and tell them that together they will first create this part of the document. Show more than one figure, even though each may not mirror the grade your group teaches; they can benefit from seeing other examples. Explain that the "Year-at-a-Glance," as the name implies, highlights mostly representative topics, unit themes, core literature, and projects throughout the year. It is important to point out that what follows the "Year-at-a-Glance" is the comprehensive portion of the Curriculum Year Overview project that they skimmed in Step Two. Detailing each unit is what forms the significant basis of your work together. Later, you will all tackle that essential portion of the project, but the "Year-at-a-Glance" is what will be the focus now.

2. Have copies of the appropriate **_"Year-at-a-Glance" templates_** available for the subjects your group teaches. These are found in the Appendix: "Year-at-a-Glance Template for Multi-Subjects" (Figure A), "Year-at-a-Glance: Language Arts" (Figure B), or "Year-at-a-Glance" blank for any subject (Figure C). Note that the templates show the months at the top of each column and the subject areas down the left side like Figure 2.1 (second grade) from this chapter. Point out, though, that placement of months and subjects is arbitrary, so it doesn't matter which is listed horizontally or vertically. The preference is really stylistic, and the finished product is not at all affected by this minor point.

3. Based on the conversation stemming from the review of content standards from one discipline, **_record representative topics, themes, core literature, and major projects_** in designated months for the subjects teachers teach in the "Year-at-a-Glance" template. Instead of writing on the template, recreate it on your computer and type in the information. I use Microsoft Word for Windows and format a table; Excel also works well. **_Make these points while completing this exercise:_**

- As you discuss and complete this "Year-at-a-Glance," tell teachers to think about the *future* and what they would want their year to look like. This is not a recording of what was done this year or in past years that didn't go over so well. And it is important to know that it is a work-in-progress.
- Note that themes are listed at the top of each column along with the months of study in Figure 2.1 (second grade). Not *every* lesson within the month focuses on these themes, but the themes are a significant part of

Figure 2.12 Concepts Table

CONCEPTS

Science	Social Studies	Math
Adaptability	Caste System	Estimation
Change	Change	Measurement
Energy	Civilization	Number
Environment	Conflict	Order
Evolution	Culture	Pattern
Gravity	Diversity	Proportions
Magnetism	Economy	Ratio
Organism	Exploration	Statistics/Probability
Scale and Structure	Geography/Climate	Symmetry
Scientific Method	Government Systems	
Systems	Immigration/Migration	
Temperature	Interdependence	
	Justice	
	Transportation	
Visual Arts	**Language Arts**	**Health**
Aesthetic	Cause/Effect	Diet
Balance	Change	Disease
Color	Character	Drugs
Contrast	Conflict	Hygiene
Form	Literal/Figurative	Illness
Line	Motivation	Nutrition
Pattern	Patterns	Wellness
Perspective	Persuasion	
Shadow	Point of View	
Shape	Purpose	
Texture	Stereotype	
Unity	Theme	

MACROCONCEPTS (broad, interdisciplinary concepts)

Change	Interdependence	Pattern
Community	Movement	Perspective
Identity	Order	Structure
		System

the month, regardless of whether some math lessons, for example, are not tied into it. You might need to revisit Figure 2.12 for a list of concepts.

- In Figure 2.3 (eighth grade), concepts and themes are listed for each social studies and science unit of study to provide cohesion for the representative topics taught. For example, "Government Systems" is a concept for these topics to be covered: documents, U.S. Constitution, Articles of Confederation, major debates, and political philosophy.

- Depending on what teachers teach, you may record other information beyond topics and skills, as shown in Figures 2.1, 2.2, and 2.3. For example, you will find that language arts teachers recorded core literature and major writing assignments.

- As you work with the content standards for each discipline that teachers in your group teach, you will continue to complete the template. Remember that the content standards are not recorded on the "Year-at-a-Glance," just the key points as shown in the examples. Entering content standards is part of the detail in Step Five.

- Once the "Year-at-a-Glance" is done, you will lead teachers in the detailed work of outlining monthly units. Know that you can always come back and review the "Year-at-a-Glance," so what you record is not set in stone.

4. ***Continue to work on filling in the "Year-at-a-Glance" template*** using the notes from Step Three, in which teachers perused and annotated standards. Emphasize that the group is merely planting seeds for the significant work ahead of identifying unit guiding questions, skills, assessments, and so on for each unit. Reviewing standards and sketching out the broad overview on the "Year-at-a-Glance" pages lays the groundwork for these unit details to follow. Once the "Year-at-a-Glance" is sketched out to the group's satisfaction, continue with Step Five, knowing that you will probably return to make modifications.

STEP FIVE: Beginning the Curriculum Year Overview Monthly Units

1. ***Print a copy for each participant of the "Year-at-a-Glance"*** that was a result of the work from Step Four. This document will serve as a reference as you detail each monthly unit during the CYO process.

2. ***Refer back to the samples of monthly curriculum units*** you showed to your group during Step Two (Figures 2.4 to 2.8). You can make copies or have extra books on hand to show them. These are samples you were to have specifically selected to closely resemble your group of teachers' particular teaching assignments by grade (or similar grade), single-subject, thematic teaching, and so forth. ***Point to elements that are included in the format*** and briefly ***explain each one*** as shown below:

- ***Unit title:*** organizational feature with theme/concept and representative topic (e.g., "How Plants Grow and Change: Sunflowers," "Government Systems: The Constitution as Law of the Land," or "The Holocaust: Tolerance vs. Intolerance").

- ***Timing:*** month or timeframe of unit.

- ***Unit guiding questions:*** list of in-depth, thought-provoking questions that serve to focus the unit and guide instruction.
- ***Standards:*** state, school, or district content standards for subject areas; in a thematically driven format, standards from several content areas will be included as they relate to a featured theme or topic; in single-subject classrooms, standards specific to the given subject are included.
- ***Skills:*** list of what skills students are to master; skills begin with a verb to describe what students need to learn and do from teacher-directed lessons.
- ***Assessments:*** identification of ongoing assessments; reference of culminating assessments after a comprehensive unit of study.
- ***Resources:*** list of materials and resources necessary for the unit.

3. Make copies of Figure D in the Appendix, a ***blank template for monthly units***. Re-create the template on your computer by formatting a table. Your goal is to fill in the components step by step as you lead targeted discussions and record information about each unit.

4. ***Record the unit (theme/concept), grade, and timing at the top of the template.*** Then ***record the content standards*** covered for this particular unit of study. You can access the content standards directly from your laptop if you have preloaded them, or use Internet access and connect to the Web site for your state's department of education, and then cut and paste them into your document. See the Bibliography for a list of Web sites. As I mentioned earlier, preloading school, state, or district standards onto your computer is the easier and more reliable method than downloading standards from a Web site while you are meeting with teachers.

5. If teachers teach a single subject, ***there might be multiple content standards*** in the first column as shown in the template. This could be true for single-subject teachers who teach on an interdisciplinary team. They might collaborate to produce this document, so several content standards will be listed as a compilation of what several teachers address for an integrated unit of study. Also, single-subject teachers might break out their content standards and list them in column one. For example, language arts teachers can divide reading, writing, speaking, and listening, or math teachers might divide the various math strands (e.g., number sense, algebra and functions, geometry, and so on). These strands are listed as subtitles.

6. Teachers may prefer that the ***standards*** be ***entered directly*** on the document in their entirety as shown in my samples, ***or*** some may want a ***reference notation*** to standards so they do not have to record all of them (e.g., Number Sense 1.2; Reading 3.3). In my experience, though, most teachers seem to like having the complete standards written on the document, so they do not have to go to another source to look up exactly what the standard details.

7. Once you record the standards, you might choose to ***emphasize key words*** (e.g., skills, concepts) embedded in them by formatting, for example, with underlining or boldface type. With all the dense text in standards, putting key words in bold is helpful so that the eye goes directly to what is taught.

8. If teachers use **themes**, be sure that they are **neither too narrow nor too broad.** Suggest combining themes. For example, if a teacher conducts a mini-unit on apples and another on trees, combine them so that "The Growth of Trees" or "The Life Cycle of Trees" represents the overarching thematic unit.

9. **Remember that this CYO is the menu,** and not the specific recipes. Therefore, it does not need to be so detailed that you overlap with curriculum binders or guides that represent comprehensive units of instruction. These units are an outgrowth of this CYO document.

STEP SIX: Discussing Standards Not Addressed

After teachers have plotted those standards that they already meet, direct their attention to those standards that they highlighted as those they do not address. I will propose a variety of suggestions to help you as you lead a discussion about these unmet standards. After discussion, determine if some standards can be placed in a particular unit, or table some for further investigation.

- Sharing best practices among colleagues is an invaluable experience. It is likely that a standard that some teachers flagged as one that is not addressed is a standard that a colleague does cover. Initiate dialogue that gets teachers talking about how they actually meet standards, so teachers can learn from one another.

- Other individuals besides classroom teachers might lend a hand to teach standards. Suggest to teachers that they ask a specialist within their school to assist with a particular standard—for example, a computer specialist or librarian. In addition, you can tap into parents if they are supportive, work well with students, and have special expertise in some areas that can enhance curriculum goals.

- Teachers feel that specific standards might be better suited for a different grade. A suggestion might be to move these standards to a more appropriate grade, so that by the time students graduate, they will benefit from exposure to all the standards, but maybe in a different grade from one listed in the content standards. If this is a serious consideration, suggest that teachers broach this conversation with their administrators and form a committee to investigate possibilities. As mentioned in Chapter 1, if this is a conversation worth having, go through the proper channels and involve administration, since this is not a decision that teachers can make alone in a grade-level group. This might not be a workable solution, though, depending on school or district regulations.

- Some standards may not be met simply because teachers lack the resources or expertise to address them. If this is the case, ask your administrator for some support for time to develop materials, money for acquiring what is needed, release time to attend a workshop, and so forth. If the school's budget is insufficient, investigate alternative sources such as the PTA/PTO, local community groups (e.g., companies, clubs), school foundations, or community-funded or district grants.

STEP SEVEN: Developing Unit Guiding Questions

Guiding or essential questions help teachers to guide and focus instruction in any given unit. They serve to translate the standards and objectives in a user-friendly way, so that students understand exactly what the unit will entail, and provide teachers and students with a clearer vision of the essence of a unit. Much of what I have learned and apply about essential questions stems from the work of Jacobs, Eickson, Wiggins, and McTighe. In *Concept-Based Curriculum and Instruction: Teaching Beyond the Facts* (2002), author Lynn Erickson defines essential questions as "a critical driver for teaching and learning. They engage students in the study and create a bridge between performance-based activities and deeper, conceptual understandings." Heidi Hayes Jacobs (1997), in *Mapping the Big Picture: Integrating Curriculum and Assessment K–12*, states: "When a teacher or group of teachers selects a question to frame and guide curricular design, it is a declaration of intent. In a sense you are saying, 'This is our focus for learning. I will put my teaching skills into helping my students examine the key concept implicit in the essential question.' "

1. In this step of the process, you will **introduce teachers to guiding questions** and facilitate designing them for each unit. Point to the CYO samples in Chapter 4 that feature these questions. Mention that teachers can create unit guiding questions for all subject areas. Before they can design their own—or critique existing ones—they need to understand what guiding questions are and why they are so critical for effective teaching and learning. The following will aid you as you train teachers about this essential teaching component.

2. ***Explain that teachers are magnets for finding and creating compelling and thought-provoking activities.*** There are activities and lessons everywhere—on Internet sites, in educational journals, in teachers' editions of textbooks, in published guides, from colleagues, and those that teachers create. I have worked with many teachers who can easily describe a multitude of activities they have taught in their classrooms. Ask teachers to recite a list of activities or lessons they do for a particular unit. Share this partial list of activities a teacher might conduct for Earth Day, either orally or visually on butcher paper or overhead:

- Visit a local beach or park and clean up the debris.
- Tour a local recycling plant.
- Collect recyclable materials in various classrooms at school.
- Separate various discarded materials and determine which are garbage and which are recyclable.
- Show pictures of the negative effects of the environmental abuse; compare with pristine environment; note differences.
- Respond to a writing prompt: "What can you do to help the earth?"

3. Share with teachers that ***students would glean much more and develop enduring understandings if all these activities were conducted within the framework of overarching guiding questions.*** To illustrate, for Earth Day activities a couple of unit guiding questions could be: *Why is it important to take care of the earth? How can we participate in taking care of the earth?* It fosters more powerful learning experiences if teachers use guiding questions for a unit of study so that students are constantly reminded of why they are doing each activity.

4. ***Each unit guiding question becomes the focus for one or several activities or lessons.*** If they are posted in the classroom, teachers can repeatedly refer to them as they state the day's objective. For example, "Today is our field trip to the beach, and we will clean up unwanted debris. Our focus for this activity is to answer the question '*How can we participate in taking care of the earth?*'" Prior to this field trip, teachers can brainstorm with students the ways in which they can take care of the earth. They can read various articles and books that illustrate caring for the earth. There are also subsets of questions that can be posed and that will undoubtedly arise during discussion. For example, during the brainstorming activity related to this guiding question, students can probe answers to: "What would the earth look like if no one took care of it? What would be the effects?" Each activity or lesson is clearly articulated to kids through the appropriate guiding question. Encourage other spin-off questions as long as students see the overarching concept you are trying to teach through the essential unit question.

5. ***Share*** with teachers what McTighe and Wiggins refer to as ***essential questions and unit questions*** in their book *Understanding by Design* (1998). They write: "Unit questions are more subject- and topic-specific and therefore better suited for framing particular content and inquiry, leading to the often more subtle essential questions. . . . It is important to note that the distinctions between essential and unit questions are not categorically pure, not black and white. Instead, they should be viewed as residing along a continuum of specificity as shades of gray. The point is not to quibble about whether a given question is an essential or a unit question, but rather to focus on its larger purposes—to frame the learning, engage the learner, link to more specific or more general questions, and guide the exploration and uncovering of important ideas." At this point in the process, you will work with teachers to frame unit guiding questions.

6. There are many ways to craft guiding questions. Lynn Erickson explains a process in Chapter 3 of her book *Concept-Based Curriculum and Instruction: Teaching Beyond the Facts* (2002) that you might read. I assist teachers to design guiding questions by ***facilitating the following exercise using standards as a guide.*** Figure 2.13, "Guiding Questions," shows the result of the exercise, as follows.

- *Paraphrase the information* in Step Seven by: (a) defining unit guiding questions as explained above; (b) stressing the importance of guiding questions in a sound educational program; and, (c) providing various examples shown in the sample detailed units in Chapter 4.
- *Explain that the task at hand* is to design unit guiding questions or critique existing guiding questions.
- *Show Figure 2.13* and explain that at the end of the exercise, teachers will have a set of unit guiding questions for targeted units.
- *Prepare a two-column table* in which the standards for a given unit are listed on one side. Leave the other column for guiding questions blank. (see Figure 2.13 as a sample for formatting). Or instruct participants to view standards for a unit and have scratch paper available.

Figure 2.13   Unit Guiding Questions

STRUCTURE AND FUNCTION OF CELLS AND ORGANISMS (LIFE SCIENCES)

McREL Standards	Unit Guiding Questions
• Knows that all organisms are composed of cells, which are the fundamental units of life; most organisms are single cells, but other organisms (including humans) are multicellular • Knows that cells convert energy obtained from food to carry on the many functions needed to sustain life • Knows the levels of organization in living systems, including cells, tissues, organs, organ systems, whole organisms, ecosystems, and the complementary nature of structure and function at each level • Knows that multicellular organisms have a variety of specialized cells, tissues, organs, and organ systems that perform specialized functions	1. How do cells function similarly in all living organisms? 2. How are plant and animal cells organized? 3. How and why do cells divide? 4. How do cells perform different roles in organisms?

FRACTIONS/MIXED NUMBERS

McREL Standards	Unit Guiding Questions
• Understands the relative magnitude and relationships among whole numbers, fractions, and mixed numbers • Adds and subtracts simple fractions • Uses models (e.g., number lines) to identify, order, and compare numbers • Uses a variety of strategies to understand problem situations (e.g., modeling problem with diagrams or physical objects)	1. How can a whole be divided into equal parts? 2. How can fractions and whole numbers be expressed in different ways? 3. How can we add and subtract different fractions and mixed numbers? 4. How are division and fractions related? 5. How do I use fractions and mixed numbers in my life? 6. How do people use fractions and mixed numbers in the world?

EARLY EXPLORATION

McREL Standards	Unit Guiding Questions
Knows the features of the major **European explorations** that took place between the 15th and 17th centuries (e.g., routes and motives of Spanish, Dutch, and English explorers; the goals and achievements of major expeditions; problems encountered on the high seas; fears and superstitions of the times; what sailors expected to find when they reached their destinations)	1. Why did Europeans choose to explore and colonize the world? 2. What were the routes and distances traveled of the major land explorers of the United States? 3. How did fears and superstitions of the times affect exploration? 4. How did explorers, sponsors, and leaders of key European expeditions overcome obstacles and accomplish their goals? 5. How did sailors react when they reached their destinations?

THE POWER OF POETRY

McREL Standards	Unit Guiding Questions
• Identifies descriptive language that clarifies and enhances ideas (e.g., figurative language, sensory images, and comparisons) • Understands the effects of author's style and complex literary devices and techniques on the overall quality of work (e.g., tone; mood; figurative language; poetic elements, such as sound, imagery, personification)	1. How does figurative language enhance poetry? 2. Why do poets feel their messages are better stated in poetry rather than prose? 3. How does the use of word choice, figurative language, or other techniques convey tone or meaning in poetry?

NOTE: Standards and Benchmarks are used and/or adapted by permission of McREL. Copyright © 2004, McREL.

Reprinted from *Curriculum Mapping: A Step-by-Step Guide for Creating Curriculum Year Overviews* by Kathy Tuchman Glass. Thousand Oaks, CA: Corwin Press, www.corwinpress.com. Reproduction authorized only for the local school site or nonprofit organization that has purchased this book.

- Tell teachers that it is easy to craft questions that begin with "what." Lynn Erickson, however, suggests that guiding questions be framed to begin with "how" or "why" to prompt further thinking. As teachers write questions, they will find that the "what" questions are subsumed in the "why" or "how" questions anyway. I subscribe to Erickson's philosophy and suggest that you lead teachers to formulate *"why" and "how" guiding questions.* Share the following examples to illustrate this point. They contain a partial list of subset questions for each guiding question. Also, remind teachers that there may be one or several lessons for each guiding question, so each "what" question can become the basis for a lesson.

  > ### *Guiding Question:* **Why is most of the earth's surface salt water?**
  >
  > o What part of the earth is covered in salt water?
  > o What are the major oceans?
  >
  > ### *Guiding Question:* **How does your community get water?**
  >
  > o What is your local community?
  > o Where are the local water sources?

- Working independently, have each teacher *brainstorm "why" and "how" questions* for each set of standards. After each teacher is finished, lead a *sharing exercise* around the table. *Determine which* of the questions would *typify the* essence of the unit and lead to enduring understandings—or create new ones from those contributed.
- For each unit of study, your goal is to craft *no more than six questions.* Five is better. *Each question should be written for students as the audience,* so make sure that the language suits them. Teachers do not want students to struggle with words in each question. An exception to this is if you are teaching a term that students will learn and use repeatedly in the unit like *imagery* or *mitosis. Come to a consensus about the list of unit guiding questions.*
- *Put these unit guiding questions in an order that makes sense for teaching.* The least complex questions are listed first and the most difficult come last.

7. Provide teachers with the following **suggestions for what they might do with guiding questions** once they are written.
   - *Post the questions* for students to see, since they serve to guide the unit. This is why questions should be written in student-friendly language.
   - Suggest that teachers *lead a brainstorming session* with students in which they provide the topic of study, and students provide a series of questions they would like to have answered during the unit. Teachers can then review the student-generated list of questions and include any noteworthy ones as part of the guiding questions, or ensure that lessons are conducted that include answers to salient questions. Teachers can even provide interest-based, differentiated opportunities for certain students to respond to questions posed and share what they gleaned with the class to enhance the unit.
   - *Pose the questions at the outset of a unit* as a vehicle for pre-assessment. In reviewing student responses to these questions, teachers collect

information from students, including what they already know. Even if they don't know the answers, teachers can determine higher-level thinking as students attempt to respond to them. This pre-assessment information will assist teachers as they create differentiated units.

- *Use the questions to frame one or a series of activities.* As teachers progress through the unit, they highlight a specific question and conduct lessons and activities geared to answering it.
- *Create culminating assessments around answering these questions,* because they represent the crux of teaching. This is one reason I include unit guiding questions on the Curriculum Year Overview, so they are present for teachers as they plan units with assessments in mind and pace their year-long curriculum.

STEP EIGHT: Identifying Skills and Accompanying Assessments

It is important for teachers to identify what they expect students to actually do and show to demonstate learning. By carefully delineating skills, teachers can develop curriculum that has a more targeted focus. Some content standards can help teachers to arrive at skills. Once these skills are pinpointed, teachers need to define what evidence students have of acquiring skills by identifying assessments.

1. Explain to teachers that ***effectively written skills show the knowledge that students acquire beyond the facts.*** They begin with a verb, but not just any verb. For example, the verb *understand* does not concretely denote what skill teachers want students to attain. However, action verbs such as *compare/contrast* or *define* provide teachers with a clearer understanding of their goals for students.

2. ***Share the following examples of skills*** to help guide teachers during this exercise. They are from various subject areas. More examples of skills are found in the document samples.

- Interpret graphs and analyze data
- Compare/contrast two systems of government
- Summarize current events
- Build a proper scale model of the schoolyard
- Construct a model of a DNA double helix
- Identify the similarities and differences among plant, animal, and bacteria cells
- Brainstorm effects of global warming
- Retell a story in logical sequence
- Find and underline examples of simile
- Define vocabulary and write using terms correctly
- Write from the point of view of a character in the story
- Critique a play
- Group objects according to shape

3. To ***write their own skills***, instruct teachers to review the content standards for a particular unit and identify the skills they want students to attain. Also, remind them of the guiding questions that are an outgrowth of the standards and represent the essence of the unit. They can ask themselves: *What should students be able to do to achieve this body of knowledge expressed in the standard or guiding question?* To assist with listing skills, teachers can also turn to the teachers' editions of their textbooks, a teacher resource guide, or other materials for a curriculum unit.

They can also use lists of verbs to help generate skills. *Bloom's Taxonomy* (1956), with its levels of cognitive domain, is a great resource because it lists a multitude of verbs. Figure 2.14 lists verbs based on Bloom's Taxonomy that you can share with teachers to assist them in developing their skill statements.

4. Teachers need to know that for skills listed (with the exception of some yearly ongoing ones), they will **conduct a formal lesson** to assist students in mastering them. For example, if a targeted skill is to *compare and contrast the daily lives of colonists in the southern colonies,* teachers will lead a formal lesson on comparing and contrasting. This might begin with comparing and contrasting something simplistic to introduce a Venn diagram, then continuing with social studies reading materials and illustrations to compare and contrast the subject of study using this organizer.

5. Once skills are identified and listed, teachers need to **determine and record the assessments** that show that students are accountable to mastering skills. Assessments are a combination of **ongoing** (formative) and **culminating** (summative), **informal and formal.** Observing students as they participate in a small-group or class discussion provides teachers with information about how students have acquired a given skill through an informal method. Informal assessments do not necessarily prove that all students have achieved a level of proficiency, but they can certainly provide useful information about students' learning. Assessments that require students to create an outline or write a paragraph are more formal. Formal assessments usually take the form of a culminating project or an exam (summative). A combination of the two is powerful for an extensive unit of study. Ongoing assessments in which teachers monitor and assess student progress throughout a unit are equally valuable. Various assessments should occur in a classroom and can be documented in the Curriculum Year Overview. Multiple forms of assessments are needed to ensure the level of proficiency that teachers expect. In addition, have teachers record any schoolwide, districtwide, and state assessments. For example, a district mandate might include issuing three writing prompts each year; teachers need to record these types of assessments, too.

6. In the following columns are some **examples of assessments**, but also review the assessments in the samples earlier in this chapter and in Chapter 4 to aid you in directing teachers in this exercise. Instruct teachers to look at each skill and ask themselves: *What informal or formal assessment might I administer that shows evidence that students are proficient in a particular skill?*

- Student participation in class discussion
- Involvement in small-group tasks and discussions
- Homework assignments
- Entries in journals or logs
- Venn diagrams
- Written summary scored against a rubric
- Analytical essay response
- District math prompt scored against a rubric
- Formal presentation scored against student-generated criteria
- Reading response notes
- Graphic organizer
- Drawing with sentence captions
- PowerPoint presentation
- Mini-dictionary of foreign language terms and their usages
- Objective test

Figure 2.14 Verbs Based on *Bloom's Taxonomy*

KNOWLEDGE		COMPREHENSION		APPLICATION	
alphabetize	quote	account	moderate	adopt	illustrate
arrange	recall	account for	offer	apply	interpret
check	recite	advance	outline	avail	make use of
choose	recognize	alter	paraphrase	build	manipulate
count	record	annotate	predict	calculate	map
define	repeat	associate	project	capitalize on	mobilize
draw	reproduce	calculate	propose	chart	operate
find	reset	change	qualify	complete	practice
group	say	construe	rephrase	compute	put in
hold	select	contemplate	report	consume	put to use
identify	show	contrive	restate	demonstrate	relate
implement	site	convert	retell	devote	schedule
know	sort	describe	review	dramatize	sketch
label	spell	discuss	reword	employ	solve
list	tabulate	estimate	scheme	examine	teach
locate	tally	expand	spell out	exercise	try
match	tell	explain	submit	exert	use
memorize	touch	expound	substitute	exploit	utilize
name	transfer	express	summarize	generate	wield
offer	underline	infer	transform	handle	
omit	write	interpret	translate		
pick		locate	vary		
point to					

ANALYSIS		SYNTHESIS		EVALUATION	
analyze	explain	arrange	generate	arbitrate	judge
appraise	group	assemble	hypothesize	appraise	justify
audit	identify	build	imagine	argue	measure
break down	include	combine	integrate	assess	prioritize
categorize	inspect	compile	invent	choose	rank
check	investigate	compose	manage	classify	rate
compare	look into	conceive	organize	conclude	recommend
contrast	order	conceptualize	plan	critique	resolve
criticize	question	construct	prepare	decide	score
debate	reason	create	prescribe	determine	select
deduce	relate	design	produce	editorialize	test
detect	screen	develop	propose	evaluate	verify
diagram	search	devise	reorder	give opinion	weigh
differentiate	separate	forecast	reorganize	grade	alternatives
discriminate	sequence	formulate	specify		
dissect	simplify	generalize	structure		
distinguish	survey				
divide	test				
examine	uncover				
experiment					

STEP NINE: Listing Resources

In *The Parallel Curriculum* by Carol Ann Tomlinson et al. (2001), the authors define resources in the following way: "Resources are materials that support learning during the teaching and learning activities. Exemplary resources are varied in format and link closely to the learning goals, students' reading and comprehension levels, and learning preferences."

1. Provide teachers with the ***definition of resources.***

2. ***Instruct teachers to brainstorm a list of various resources*** they use in their classrooms. Generate this list on an easel so that they can easily see it. Here is a partial list of entries to share if teachers need prodding: state-adopted textbooks, picture books, primary source material, maps and globes, posters, short stories or poems, lab demonstration, guest speakers, artwork, and computer software. Review the CYO samples from this chapter and Chapter 4 and include resources listed there, as well.

3. Focusing on one unit at a time, have teachers ***identify the resources*** they use to assist them in teaching it. Encourage them to input the proper bibliographic information for textbooks and books, so that any teacher who is unfamiliar with the resources can find them. I sometimes even include chapter and page numbers to make it easier for teachers when they begin a unit. Especially for textbook references, teachers appreciate the inclusion of specific chapters and page numbers, since the texts are often massive. Because textbooks are frequently revised, it would also be helpful to reference the copyright dates in your document. Identifying resources also means that teachers input materials that a colleague has or resources housed in a certain school location (e.g., library or storage cabinet). In parentheses next to specific resources, identify these locations so teachers know to whom and where to go to borrow them.

4. Teachers will no doubt realize that they need additional resources that they currently do not have available. Suggest that they ***list resources that they need*** to acquire, such as specific curriculum or additional books. Later, they can determine the best way to acquire these materials.

5. ***If your group does not want to include ongoing programs as defined in Step Ten, then go to Step Eleven next.*** Read Step Ten yourself, and then present this option to teachers to allow them to decide whether or not to include ongoing programs. After all, it is their document and needs to serve their purposes.

STEP TEN: Identifying Ongoing Instruction or Projects

Not all curriculum maps that you might have seen include ongoing instruction or projects conducted or issued on a routine basis (daily, weekly, quarterly, and so on). However, some teachers with whom I collaborate to produce this document like to include them, because they form a significant part of their instructional program. This step includes an explanation of what ongoing projects or routines entail, and how you might direct teachers to include them if they so desire.

1. Throughout the school day, week, month, or quarter, ***teachers might assign ongoing projects or conduct certain routines*** that are an essential part of instruction in one or several subject areas. For example, a kindergarten teacher might have a sharing program in which students bring in an object to share that begins with a featured letter of the week. Or the ongoing program might be guided reading daily or three times a week for primary-grade students. In an upper elementary math class, students might do a graphing exercise as part of a weekly routine. Social studies teachers of any grade might assign a weekly historical journal calling for students to write from the perspective of someone living long ago. And in science, students might be asked to keep an observational journal each day or respond to a summary writing prompt at the end of a unit. The opportunities for ongoing programs are endless.

2. It might be beneficial for some teachers to include a ***reference*** to these ***ongoing programs*** in their CYO and insert them in appropriate sections of the document binder or at the beginning, behind the "Year-at-a-Glance." Some teachers prefer more detailed references about these ongoing programs than others, but that is a personal choice.

3. ***Refer teachers to the examples*** in Figures 2.15 to 2.18 for these ongoing programs. If teachers do not teach a subject or grade of a given sample, suggest that they take a look at their format and content, which may be useful, and adapt as needed. The standards listed are from McREL, but teachers can easily make connections between their own standards and those listed. Some pages are for teachers; others pages are student checklists. Teachers can include either or both types in their documents, with the more detailed instructions and curriculum housed in curriculum binders or file folders. Encourage teachers to create a rubric for assessing the work that students do for a particular ongoing program, as appropriate. Record any ongoing programs that your teachers wish to include in their document after discussion and review of these samples.

- *Figure 2.15: "Multi-Subject Daily Journals"* includes language arts and math journal activities that a teacher might issue each week.
- *Figure 2.16: "Weekly Vocabulary Writing Checklist":* During the week, students define a list of words, identify Greek and Latin roots, and satisfy assignments (e.g., categorizing, classifying, making analogies, and so on) in order to learn the words. Each Friday, students complete the assignment shown on the checklist as a culminating writing piece. The expectation is that they exhibit how well they can actually use targeted vocabulary, both grammatically and in context, while writing on a topic of their choice. This checklist can certainly be adapted to meet the developmental needs of individual students. Some students might elect to write a chapter each week so that by the end of the semester they have a novel. Others might be given fewer words that are less complex.
- *Figure 2.17: "Science Summary Checklist"* is an alternative to having students answer questions at the end of each science chapter or unit. The goal is for students to exhibit knowledge and understanding of the chapter or unit by following the points listed on the

checklist. As with the vocabulary checklist, teachers may extend or modify this checklist based on students' abilities.

- *Figure 2.18: "Book Projects":* A common assignment in language arts classrooms is for students to read a novel independently and then create a book project at the end of the month, quarter, or trimester. The "Book Projects" sheet shows the standards that upper elementary grade teachers use as a guide for an independent reading program.
- In Chapter 4, additional routines are included for primary grades only; see the section called "Primary Daily Routine Examples."

4. *After including any ongoing programs, the draft of the document is almost complete at this point.* Continue to Step Eleven for direction on articulation with other grade-level teachers in like subject areas.

STEP ELEVEN: Articulating Across Grade Levels

Remind teachers that the Curriculum Year Overview they have created to this point is the basic, balanced menu of offerings. Some teacher groups create one that is more detailed than others, but nevertheless it is a menu of the basic food groups only. So far, teachers have worked with grade-level groups. Now is a good time to introduce Chapter 3 and determine if your group is ready to articulate across subject areas from grade to grade. If they are not so inclined now, this is something to plan for in the future, since the balanced meal of chicken, rice, and broccoli (the curriculum units) is more well rounded with appetizers and desserts (other grades' standards and expectations). It is a stronger, more comprehensive menu when items other than the basic food groups are included. In Chapter 3, I present a continuum that teachers across subject areas can create that allows for widespread articulation to guide instruction. By articulating clearly within a subject area spanning grades, teachers can uncover gaps and unnecessary repetition in the curriculum. Teachers can then step back and make professional decisions regarding curriculum to improve how they serve the students.

If teachers are not yet ready to embark upon articulation at this point, finish any formatting, and then send it electronically and on disk to all teachers and administrators involved in the project. Even if now is not the best time for teachers to articulate across grades using the suggestions in Chapter 3 (or something similar), then encourage them to commit to a future time when they will tackle this necessary step. Emphasize that the Curriculum Year Overview will not be as useful and powerful a document if it is restricted only to isolated grades. It is imperative that all teachers across grades come together at some point and examine their subject-specific content critically and thoughtfully to avoid repetition and unnecessary overlap of content and instruction, and determine areas that are left omitted.

Step Twelve—"Piloting and Revising the Document"—is critical to the success and future use of the curriculum map. Continue with this last step in the process.

Figure 2.15   Weekly Program: Multi-Subject Daily Journals

Weekly Program: Multi-Subject Daily Journals

	McREL Standards	Descriptions of Journal Activities
LANGUAGE ARTS **WOW (Word of the Week):** **Vocabulary Development**	**Reading Standards:** • Uses word origins and derivations to understand word meaning • Uses a variety of context clues to decode unknown words • Uses word reference materials (e.g., dictionary, thesaurus) to determine the meaning, pronunciation, and derivations of unknown words **Writing Standards:** • Uses strategies to write for a variety of purposes and different audiences • Uses descriptive language that clarifies and enhances ideas • Uses paragraph form in writing • Uses grammatical and conventions of spelling, capitalization, and punctuation in writing	• Students learn a word each week during a teacher-generated weekly program called WOW (Word of the Week). Program overview: ○ Each **Monday,** students are given a WOW sentence that includes a new vocabulary word(s). They predict meanings using context clues. ○ Words are differentiated by readiness, so students typically have different words and numbers of words to work with each week. ○ Students use a dictionary to confirm meanings, do syllabification, find other forms of the words and word origins, use words in new sentences, use a thesaurus to find antonyms and synonyms, find Greek and Latin roots. • All words are posted in the room and used frequently in writing, speaking, and listening. • Each week, students select words from their lists and create writing that incorporates these vocabulary words. Students choose the type of writing.
MATH **MYTM (Make You Think Math):** **Problem Solving**	**Mathematical Reasoning:** • Uses a variety of strategies to understand problem situation • Represents problem situation in a variety of forms • Understands that some ways of representing a problem are more helpful than others • Uses trial and error and the process of elimination to solve problems • Uses explanations of the methods and reasoning behind the problem's solution to determine reasonableness of and to verify results with respect to the original problem	• Content: Students are assigned word problems each **Tuesday** that require critical thinking skills. It may be a deeper application of a current math lesson, a problem related to a MYTM problem from previous week, or a problem to assist students in how to reada math problem. • Students respond to their MYTM prompts in their daily journals.
LANGUAGE ARTS **Analyzing Quote**	**Reading Standards:** • Uses word origins and derivations to understand word meaning • Understands the author's purpose or point of view • Paraphrases information in quotes • Makes inferences based on explicit and implicit information in quotes **Writing Standards:** • Uses strategies to write for a variety of purposes and different audiences • Uses descriptive language that clarifies and enhances ideas • Uses paragraph form in writing • Uses grammatical conventions of spelling, capitalization, and punctuation in writing	• QOW—Quote of the Week • Each **Wednesday,** students interpret a quote presented by the teacher and make personal connections. • Teacher presents brief overview of quote originator. • Students write quote responses in their daily journals.

NOTE: Standards and Benchmarks are used and/or adapted by permission of McREL. Copyright © 2004, McREL.

Reprinted from *Curriculum Mapping: A Step-by-Step Guide for Creating Curriculum Year Overviews* by Kathy Tuchman Glass. Thousand Oaks, CA: Corwin Press, www.corwinpress.com. Reproduction authorized only for the local school site or nonprofit organization that has purchased this book.

Figure 2.16   *Weekly Vocabulary Writing Checklist*

Weekly Vocabulary Writing Checklist

Name: _____

You will create a story that correctly and creatively incorporates at least <u>seven</u> of this week's vocabulary words. Feel free to use words from earlier weeks, too. Use this checklist as a guide while writing.

IDEAS and CONTENT

☐ **MAIN IDEA:** I develop one clear, main idea without getting off track. I follow the guidelines of this assignment.

☐ **DETAILS:** I use specific and interesting details in my story.

☐ **ORIGINALITY:** I try to write an original story.

ORGANIZATION

☐ **STORYLINE:** My story has a compelling beginning, middle, and end.

☐ **SEQUENCING:** My details are in just the right order so sequencing is logical and effective.

☐ **TRANSITIONS BETWEEN MAIN IDEAS:** I use thoughtful transitions to connect main ideas from paragraph to paragraph.

☐ **PARAGRAPHING:** I make sure to indent new paragraphs.

☐ **TITLE:** I include an original title.

WORD CHOICE

☐ **VOCABULARY USAGE:** I use all vocabulary words appropriately in a grammatical sense.

☐ **VOCABULARY WORDS:** I show that I know each word's meaning through my writing.

VOICE

☐ **POINT OF VIEW:** I maintain a consistent point of view (1st or 3rd person) throughout my story.

☐ **AUDIENCE/PURPOSE:** I write with a clear sense of audience and purpose.

SENTENCE FLUENCY

☐ **SENTENCE VARIETY:** I vary my sentence structure between simple, compound, and complex sentences.

☐ **SENTENCE BEGINNINGS:** I vary my sentence beginnings so not all sentences begin in the same way.

☐ **TRANSITIONS:** I use appropriate transitions from sentence to sentence.

☐ **FRAGMENTS/RUN-ONS:** I have no fragments or run-ons.

CONVENTIONS

☐ **SPELLING:** My vocabulary words are spelled correctly; grade-level words are also spelled correctly.

☐ **PUNCTUATION:** Punctuation is accurate.

☐ **CAPITALIZATION:** I capitalize appropriate words correctly.

☐ **GRAMMAR:** My grammar is correct.

☐ **NEATNESS:** My writing is legible and my paper is neat.

Copyright © 2007 by Corwin Press. All rights reserved. Reprinted from *Curriculum Mapping: A Step-by-Step Guide for Creating Curriculum Year Overviews,* by Kathy Tuchman Glass. Thousand Oaks, CA: Corwin Press, www.corwinpress.com. Reproduction authorized only for the local school site or nonprofit organization that has purchased this book.

Figure 2.17   Science Summary Checklist

Science Summary Checklist

Name: _____

You will write a summary of our current science unit on _____.

IDEAS/CONTENT and ORGANIZATION

☐ I **satisfy this entire assignment** as listed on this checklist.

☐ My writing is **thoughtful** and **clearly shows I understand the material.**

☐ I write a **three-paragraph summary** of this current science reading selection with this format:

1st Paragraph:
☐ I clearly define the **main idea** of this science concept.

2nd Paragraph:
☐ I **support the main idea** with at least **three significant details.**

☐ One detail is in **my own words.**

☐ The second detail is **a direct quote** from the book with an explanation.

☐ The third detail is in **my own words or a direct quote with explanation.**

3rd Paragraph:
☐ I write about how this **main idea is or can be significant** to my life.

WORD CHOICE

☐ I use **specific and accurate scientific terms.**

☐ My paper **does not include repetition or unclear language.**

CONVENTIONS

☐ I use **appropriate capital letters.**

☐ I use **correct punctuation.** I make sure to use **quotation marks** correctly when quoting from the book.

☐ I **spell** all words correctly. I use the dictionary for words I do not know how to spell.

☐ My writing is **legible.** It looks like I took care of my paper because it is **neat,** too.

☐ My sentences make sense and do not have **grammatical** errors.

SENTENCE FLUENCY

☐ I write **complete sentences and do not include run-ons.**

☐ For example, I begin with various transitions, subjects, or even adverbs to **vary my sentence structure.**

☐ **My sentence beginnings vary.** Some sentences begin with subjects and others begin with dependent clauses.

Copyright © 2007 by Corwin Press. All rights reserved. Reprinted from *Curriculum Mapping: A Step-by-Step Guide for Creating Curriculum Year Overviews,* by Kathy Tuchman Glass. Thousand Oaks, CA: Corwin Press, www.corwinpress.com. Reproduction authorized only for the local school site or nonprofit organization that has purchased this book.

Figure 2.18   Book Projects

Book Projects

Each quarter, students read books independently from a teacher- or student-generated list of books; after reading, students complete a project with a clear set of criteria; projects may sometimes be presented to the whole class; all of these standards will be met at year's end and used to assist with criteria and assessment; individual projects will not include all of these standards at once.

McREL STANDARDS

Reading
- Monitors own reading strategies and makes modifications as needed
- Uses a variety of context clues to decode unknown words
- Knows the defining characteristics of a variety of literary forms and genres
- Uses personal criteria to select reading material
- Understands similarities and differences within and among literary works
- Understands the author's purpose or point of view
- Understands the basic concept of plot
- Knows themes that recur across literary works
- Makes connections between characters or simple events in a literary work and people or events in his/her own life

Writing
- Uses the strategies of the writing process: prewriting, drafting and revising, editing and publishing
- Uses strategies to write for a variety of purposes and different audiences
- Uses descriptive language that clarifies and enhances ideas
- Uses paragraph form in writing
- Uses grammatical and conventions of spelling, capitalization, and punctuation in writing

Listening and Speaking
- Uses strategies to convey a clear main point when speaking
- Makes basic oral presentations to class · Uses a variety of nonverbal communication skills
- (e.g., eye contact, gestures, facial expressions, postures)
- Uses a variety of verbal communication skills (e.g., projection, tone, volume, rate, articulation, pace, phrasing)
- Organizes ideas for oral presentations
- Understands the main ideas and supporting details in spoken texts (e.g., presentations by peers)

NOTE: Standards and Benchmarks are used and/or adapted by permission of McREL. Copyright © 2004, McREL.

Reprinted from *Curriculum Mapping: A Step-by-Step Guide for Creating Curriculum Year Overviews* by Kathy Tuchman Glass. Thousand Oaks, CA: Corwin Press. www.corwinpress.com. Reproduction authorized only for the local school site or nonprofit organization that has purchased this book.

STEP TWELVE: Piloting and Revising the Document

Present the document to teachers with the letter in Figure 2.19. You can revise the letter or use it as written. You will undoubtedly talk with teachers, as well as present the letter, so explain to them that this Curriculum Year Overview is organic. By that I mean that it takes on new shapes as teachers teach with it, try new curriculum, receive a new textbook during an adoption period, learn more professionally, change a mode of teaching, welcome a new teacher to the team, and so on. The CYO is a document that calls for revision. Therefore, it is probably misleading to call it a "finished document" because it is indeed a work-in-progress.

Teachers will pilot the document, using the units of study spelled out in the curriculum map to guide them. Encourage them to use the guiding questions, teach to specific skills, and assess student work with the document close at hand so they have ready access to what they created in the CYO. Instruct teachers to use sticky notes, red pens, highlighters, or whatever works for them to make corrections on their document. Even better, since the teachers received the document electronically and on disk, they can type the changes directly onto the document. I suggest you send reminder e-mails or notes to teachers to edit the document. Recording these changes will then reflect the actual teaching that teachers do.

After teachers have made notations, plan a meeting either at mid-year or at the end of the school year (or both) to compare and discuss all the changes teachers have made, and then make the necessary corrections. Certainly teachers will make adjustments to the document in subsequent years, but the first year of piloting involves the most changes.

This revision step is critical to maximize the effectiveness of the CYO. If teachers discover that a portion of the document does not accurately reflect their curriculum, revisions must be made on the map so that it is a true representation of their work with students. An accurate recording of their units is important for others perusing their documents and making decisions on what is written in it. For example, teachers of other grades will use the document to make professional decisions about their teaching so that there is fluidity and the right amount of depth and complexity in a unit of study. If teachers do not record changes, students are ultimately affected by repetitive or absent curriculum and instruction.

SOME FINAL THOUGHTS

The process detailed in this chapter and the guidance throughout the book serve to assist teachers in outlining their school years. There will certainly be times when teachers will experience cathartic moments and arrive at a different way of performing a process step or two. Some teachers who are invested in creating a Curriculum Year Overview prefer following each step as written, but others prefer to diverge from the process to gain more ownership of what they will produce. This is to be expected.

Figure 2.19   Dear _____,

Dear _____,

Ta dah! Here is the Curriculum Year Overview for your grade that we worked hard to compile. It is a great endorsement of all the wonderful learning that happens in your classroom. I enjoyed facilitating this project because it validates what you all do so well and also extends to what you might want to try.

Consider this document a work-in-progress. Remember that this is YOUR document to customize as you see fit to meet your needs and those of your students and to guide you during the year. Please write any changes, additions, and edits that you have directly on the document or edit the actual document that you were given electronically or by disc. We will meet again at a later date to review what you have added so the document can be revised accordingly. Our meeting will be scheduled after you have had a chance to teach with this document close at hand for a period of time. That way, you can accurately and authentically document any changes.

I definitely benefited from working on this with you and your team. I know we pulled long, arduous days together on this project. But I think once you see in the pages all that you have created, you'll see it was well worth the effort.

Call or e-mail me with any questions or comments.

Best,

Copyright © 2007 by Corwin Press. All rights reserved. Reprinted from *Curriculum Mapping: A Step-by-Step Guide for Creating Curriculum Year Overviews*, by Kathy Tuchman Glass. Thousand Oaks, CA: Corwin Press, www.corwinpress.com. Reproduction authorized only for the local school site or nonprofit organization that has purchased this book.

The outcome of your work together is to create a finished document ready to be piloted, but continually encourage dialogue among teachers and the sharing of best practices to foster forward movement along a professional continuum. In this way, the *process* of creating a CYO is just as important as the end product. This curriculum map is just one of many tools that effective educators use to make learning meaningful and memorable for students.

3

Articulation From Grade to Grade

The project of articulating across grades (Step Eleven) is a critical component of the Curriculum Year Overview, so I devote a chapter to this facet of the process. This chapter presents the format of a continuum that shows the articulation from grade to grade. The purpose of a continuum is to allow teachers to easily see what was taught in a previous year and what will be taught so they can better prepare meaningful and effective subject-area curriculum that will benefit all students. Using a continuum shows the broad picture across many grades, but each grade-level curriculum map includes the appropriate skills and strategies from the continuum. You might include the appropriate continuums in the last section of the CYO document binder so that teachers have access to information for lesson planning across all grades, in addition to their unit maps, which contain line-item information for each grade.

Examining and identifying subject-specific content from one grade to the next is essential to maximize student learning. This articulation allows teachers to:

- Avoid too much repetition.
- Address any holes where skills and concepts are mistakenly absent.
- Reinforce skills and concepts introduced in a previous grade.
- Provide a snapshot of material that will be taught in the next grade.

Teachers often view the standards as grade-specific, without the added benefit of seeing the overall scope of students' learning in a given subject area, which spans the grades. Some states have created standards documents formatted by grade clusters, so teachers can see this articulation, but this is not always the case. One comment I hear repeatedly is that the standards document lists only what teachers are to cover in a given grade level, but there is no preparation before the standard is listed, and no reinforcement in subsequent grades. This is what led me to include the continuums found in this chapter. As facilitator, (1) review the information and examples in this chapter; (2) lead a discussion about the benefits of a continuum for articulation purposes; and, (3) re-create continuums or a similar articulation format for the subjects that your group teaches, using the samples in this chapter as a guide. If your group teaches language arts, critically review each line item on the continuums and revise as needed. If your group teaches subjects other than language arts, read the last section of this chapter entitled "Continuums for Other Subject Areas" to get suggestions on leading these participants.

GRAMMAR AND CONVENTIONS CONTENT STANDARDS CONTINUUM

Although teachers of various grade levels and subjects are involved in creating a CYO, the articulation continuums I present in this chapter are in the language arts arena. There are two different continuums that span kindergarten to eighth grade: one for grammar and conventions and another for writing types, or genres. The reason for the language arts focus is that teachers may not all be well versed in the nuances of a mathematics, social studies, or science curriculum, but all are familiar with basic grammar and conventions. Furthermore, if a school's focus is on writing throughout the curriculum, the continuum for writing types will have implications across several subject areas. My hope is that by presenting two formats for areas within language arts, you can help teachers of other subject areas adapt the content for their purposes. In addition, high school teachers can extend the kindergarten-to-eighth-grade format found here to include their grade levels.

Although many language arts standards documents are sufficient in guiding teachers to perform well at teaching grammar and conventions, sometimes the standards are vague and incomplete. For example, in one particular standards document, fourth-grade students are expected to *"combine short, related sentences with participial phrases."* Unfortunately, the content standards do not state that students must be able to master *participles* in order to prepare for this fourth-grade standard. Another example of the document's lack of direction concerns *pronouns.* If teachers review a student's grammar or language handbook for *pronoun,* they will find a whole host of definitions, including personal pronouns, reflexive pronouns, possessive pronouns, indefinite pronouns, and so on. In one standards document, the direction in teaching types of pronoun is left largely to some grade-level teachers to determine, as illustrated by this excerpt:

- *First grade:* Identify and correctly use singular possessive pronouns (*my/mine, his/her, hers, your/yours*) in writing and speaking.
- *Third grade:* Identify and use pronouns correctly in writing and speaking.
- *Fifth grade:* Identify and correctly use pronouns.
- *Sixth grade:* Identify and properly use indefinite pronouns.
- *Seventh grade:* Identify and make clear references between pronouns and antecedents.

Teachers asked for more specific direction for teaching grammar and conventions than the state document provides. In response, I worked with them to create a document (Figure 3.1: "Grammar and Conventions Continuum") with more specific articulation and additional standards that reflect a one- to three-year time span of each skill or concept. Why one to three years? Some standards take three years to master; others are a one-year standard. The intent in creating such a document with an articulated time span is for teachers to: (1) avoid unnecessary repetition in teaching some skills and concepts in grade after grade; (2) help plan and deliver curriculum so there is more success in getting students proficient with particular skills or concepts; and (3) seek ownership among teachers about what they are to teach.

The "Grammar and Conventions Continuum" document (Figure 3.1) includes grammar- and conventions-specific skills with symbols, as shown in the symbol key. These symbols are placed in the appropriate grade levels for teaching and represent the hallmark of articulation. In this way, teachers know to what extent they are to teach to a standard. You will notice that some grade levels include two symbols (•/*), which means that a teacher can introduce and achieve proficiency for a particular skill in that given year. These symbols can be used for any subject area continuum.

Symbol Key:

- **•** Introduce skill, strategy, concept, and so on.
- **→** Continue to teach, knowing students received an introduction in previous year.
- **✻** Seek to gain proficiency at an intermediate level for 90% of students.

The major drawback in repeating standards year after year is that teachers have no time to get to developmental standards they are supposed to teach, so students get short-changed. The continuum clearly shows which years ***all*** teachers are invested in teaching a skill or concept. This way, the ownership is not on one grade level alone (unless it is a simplistic one-year standard), but a team effort. To master more challenging standards, students need repeated exposure and support, and the continuum keeps that goal uppermost in teachers' minds so they can plan instruction accordingly.

Figure 3.1   Grammar and Conventions Continuum for Writing

Grammar and Conventions Continuum for Writing

PRINT CONCEPTS

	K	1st	2nd	3rd	4th	5th	6th	7th	8th
Identifies letters of the alphabet	●/✳								
Uses upper- and lowercase letters of the alphabet	●	✳							
Spaces words and sentences	●	✳		NOT APPLICABLE					
Writes from left to right and from top to bottom	●	✳							
Includes margins	●	✳							

CAPITALIZATION

	K	1st	2nd	3rd	4th	5th	6th	7th	8th
Uses capitalization for first and last names	●/✳								
Uses capitalization for first word of a sentence, the pronoun *I*, and names of people	●	→	✳						
Uses capitalization for titles of people; days of the week; months of the year; heading, salutation, and the closing of letter		●	→	✳					
Uses capitalization for names of towns, cities, counties, states, and countries; names of streets; holidays; titles before names			●	✳					
Uses capitalization for titles of books, stories, poems, magazines, newspapers, songs, and works of art and the first word in quotations				●	→	✳			
Uses capitalization for proper nouns (team names, companies, schools and institutions, departments of government, religions, school subjects), proper adjectives, nationalities, brand names of products, divided quotations							●	→	✳

SYMBOL KEY: ● introduce skill, strategy, concept, etc.

→ **continue to teach knowing students received an introduction previous year**

✳ **seek to gain proficiency at an intermediate level for 90 percent of students**

SPELLING / PENMANSHIP

	K	1st	2nd	3rd	4th	5th	6th	7th	8th
Spells first and last name	●	*							
Spells high-frequency, commonly misspelled words from appropriate grade-level list				ongoing					
Spells phonetically regular words	●	→	*						
Uses letter-sound relationships	●	→	*						
Spells basic short-vowel, long-vowel, *r*-controlled, and consonant blend patterns	●	→	*						
Uses a dictionary and other resources to spell words				ongoing					
Uses initial consonant substitution to spell related words				●	→	*			
Uses vowel combinations for correct spelling				●	→	*			
Uses contractions, compounds, roots, suffixes, prefixes, and syllable construction to spell words				●	→	*			
Forms letters in print	●	→	*						
Writes in cursive				●	→	*			

SYMBOL KEY: ● **introduce skill, strategy, concept, etc.**

→ **continue to teach knowing students received an introduction previous year**

* **seek to gain proficiency at an intermediate level for 90% of students**

(Continued)

Figure 3.1 (Continued)

GRAMMAR / PARTS OF SPEECH

	K	1st	2nd	3rd	4th	5th	6th	7th	8th
VERBS:	NOT APPLICABLE								
Identifies and uses action verbs		●	→	*					
Identifies and uses past, present, and future verb tenses				●	*				
Identifies and uses simple tenses, forms of regular verbs, verbs that agree with subject				●	→	*			
Identifies and uses linking and auxiliary verbs, verb phrases, and correct forms of regular and irregular verbs				●	→	*			
Identifies and uses infinitives								*	*
PRONOUNS:									
Identifies and uses personal pronouns		●	*						
Identifies and uses first-, second-, and third-person pronouns				●	→	*			
Identifies and understands how to use subject, object, and possessive pronouns				●	→	*			
Identifies and uses demonstrative pronouns (e.g., *this, these, that, those*) and relative pronouns (e.g., *who, whom, which, whichever*)					●	→	*		
Identifies and uses reflexive pronouns (e.g., *myself, herself*) and intensive pronouns (e.g., *himself*)							●	→	*
Identifies and uses indefinite pronouns (e.g., *others, one, everyone*) and interrogative pronouns (e.g., *who, whose, what*)						●	→	*	
Identifies and uses pronouns that agree with their antecedents						●	→	*	
MISCELLANEOUS PARTS OF SPEECH:									
Identifies and uses nouns (e.g., nouns for simple objects, family members, community workers, and categories)		●	*						
Identifies and uses nouns (e.g., plural and singular naming words, forms regular and irregular plurals of nouns, uses common and proper nouns, uses nouns as subjects)				●	→	*			
Identifies and uses nouns (e.g., forms possessives of nouns; forms irregular plural nouns)							●	→	*
Identifies and uses adjectives (e.g., descriptive words)		●	*						
Identifies and uses adjectives (e.g., indefinite, numerical, predicate adjectives)				●	→	*			
Identifies and uses adjectives (e.g., positive, comparative, superlative)							●	→	*
Identifies and uses adverbs (i.e., uses words that answer how, when, where, and why)		●	*						
Identifies and uses adverbs to make comparisons; identifies and uses types of adverbs (i.e., time, place, manner)				●	→	*			
Identifies and uses adverbs (e.g., chooses between forms of adverbs such as positive, comparative, superlative degrees)							●	→	*

PARTS OF SPEECH: (Continued)

	K	1st	2nd	3rd	4th	5th	6th	7th	8th
Identifies and uses articles (i.e., *the, a, an*)				●/*					
Identifies and uses prepositions				●	→	*			
Identifies and uses interjections (e.g., *well, hey, wow, oh,* etc.)				●	→	*			
Identifies and uses participles (i.e., *an <u>embarrassing</u> moment, a <u>tired</u> uncle*)							●	*	
Identifies and uses coordinating (i.e., *for, and, nor, but, or, yet, so*) and subordinating (e.g., *although, after, because, though, etc.*) conjunctions					●	→	*		

PUNCTUATION

	K	1st	2nd	3rd	4th	5th	6th	7th	8th
COMMAS:									
Uses commas in dates and addresses and after greetings and closings of a letter		●	→	*					
Uses commas for items in a series		●	→	*					
Uses commas between city and state			●	*					
Uses commas to separate adjectives					●	*			
Uses commas to set off interjections (e.g., *well, hey, wow, oh,* etc.) and for direct address (e.g., *John, please come here.*)					●	→	*		
Understands how to use commas to set off appositives						●	*		
Uses commas with introductory phrases, dependent clauses, and with a conjunction in compound sentences					●	→	*		
Uses commas to set off dialogue in direct quotations	**(see Quotation Marks)**								
QUOTATION MARKS:									
Uses quotation marks and commas for direct quotes when writing dialogue without interruptions (i.e., *Jan said, "I love you."* OR *"I love you,"* Jan said.)			●	→	*				
Uses quotation marks and commas for interrupted quotes in dialogue and quotes within quotes (i.e., *"Please understand,"* Jan cried, *"that I love you."* AND *"I think he said 'I'm mad about you' if I'm not mistaken,"* said Joe.)						●	→	*	
Uses quotation marks around titles and when using the words of a published work				●	→	*			
COLONS:									
Uses a colon between hour and minutes			●	*					
Uses a colon to introduce a list					●	*			
Uses colons in business letters and before extended quotations								●	*

Figure 3.1 (Continued)

	K	1st	2nd	3rd	4th	5th	6th	7th	8th
MISCELLANEOUS PUNCTUATION:									
Uses periods after declarative sentences and question marks after interrogative sentences	●	→	∗						
Uses periods after imperative sentences and in initials, abbreviations, and titles before names			●	→	∗				
Uses contractions (e.g., *isn't, aren't, can't, won't*)		●	→	∗					
Uses apostrophes in possessive nouns				●	→	∗			
Uses underlining or italics to identify titles (e.g., for titles of books, magazines, plays, movies)				●	→	∗			
Uses semicolons in compound sentences between independent clauses						●	→	∗	
Uses parentheses (i.e., to add or clarify information)							●	∗	
Uses hyphens, dashes, ellipses								●	∗

SENTENCE STRUCTURE

	K	1st	2nd	3rd	4th	5th	6th	7th	8th
Uses complete sentences		●	∗						
Uses declarative, exclamatory, imperative, and interrogative sentences			●	∗					
Distinguishes between sentences and fragments			●	→	∗				
Identifies and avoids simple run-ons (e.g., *The train chugs along it will make many stops.*) and sentence fragments (e.g., *Splashed in puddles.*)			●	→	∗				
Identifies and avoids more sophisticated sentence fragments (e.g., *Because he ran over to my house*)					●	∗			
Identifies and avoids more sophisticated run-on sentences (e.g., *Playing tennis is a challenging activity it might be too exhausting to some but easier for others.*)					●	∗			
Identifies the subject and predicate of a simple sentence				●	∗				
Uses appropriate subject/verb agreement				●	∗				
Identifies and writes compound sentences; identifies the subject and predicate of a compound sentence					●	→	∗		
Uses appropriate transitions					●	∗			
Identifies and uses appropriate subject/verb agreement for compound sentences					●	→	∗		
Writes complex sentences					●	→	∗		
Writes compound-complex sentences							●	∗	
Uses participial phrases							●	→	∗
Uses appositives						●	∗		
Uses prepositional phrases					●	→	∗		
Uses parallel structure (parallelism)								●	∗
Uses appropriate pronoun/antecedent agreement						●	→	∗	
Uses dependent and independent clauses					●	→	∗		
Uses the active voice								●	∗
Uses explicit transitional devices						●	∗		

SYMBOL KEY: ● **introduce skill, strategy, concept, etc.**
→ **continue to teach knowing students received an introduction previous year**
∗ **seek to gain proficiency at an intermediate level for 90% of students**

NOTE: Standards and Benchmarks are used and/or adapted by permission of McREL. Copyright © 2004, McREL.

Reprinted from *Curriculum Mapping: A Step-by-Step Guide for Creating Curriculum Year Overviews* by Kathy Tuchman Glass. Thousand Oaks, CA: Corwin Press, www.corwinpress.com. Reproduction authorized only for the local school site or nonprofit organization that has purchased this book.

WRITING TYPES (GENRES) CONTINUUM

Articulation of writing types is beneficial, because all teachers of different grades know how to support one another to scaffold writing instruction. It is also valuable to discuss articulation if a school or district is invested in writing across the curriculum. The "Writing Types Continuum" features two versions of a document that delineates what writing types are taught per grade at a given school (or district) and the teaching expectations. These expectations are defined using a key; the two continuums use different symbol keys, as shown here:

Key Option #1

*	Comprehensive unit complete with stages of the writing process
√	Short series of lessons
s	State content standard

Key Option #2

I:	Introduction
E:	Emphasis
P:	Proficiency

If teachers choose to create such a document, recommend that they ask their administrators to devote a staff development session to this project. During this meeting, an administrator or facilitator engages in the following discussions/tasks in order to create a product tailored to the needs of teachers and students:

- Conduct a thorough inventory of what writing types are currently taught in each grade.
- Discuss what writing types are expectations of the district or state.
- Arrive at a definition of each writing type, so teachers are altogether clear about the elements involved in each writing domain; there are several definitions, so it is important to decide on one that works best for your staff; use the same textbook students read as one of your multiple resources; consistent clarity of language is also important. (See "A Note About Narrative Writing" as an example.)
- If a writing type is taught in more than one grade, determine how learning is differentiated and scaffolded to challenge students at each grade level.
- Extend the discussion to articulation across subject areas; determine which writing assignments—both formal and informal—are expectations of various content areas; create a document that reflects writing in different disciplines in addition to grade levels.

A Note About Narrative Writing

In working with teachers, we have found that there is a discrepancy when defining narrative writing content standards. If teachers are not clear about what elements are included in each narrative writing type, then surely students will not be, either. One discussion your teachers might broach centers on clear-cut definitions of the narrative writing applications (e.g., autobiography, biography, short story, personal narrative) and differences among similar narrative types, for example, *personal narrative, autobiography, personal incident, and personal memoir.*

Another major discussion point centers on which grade level has ownership for teaching the short story and the expectations for this story in terms of content and length. For example, what role should *plot* play in a short story? Plot is defined as including an *introduction/beginning (optional), central conflict, rising action, climax, falling action,* and *resolution/denouement.* Teachers might find it useful to engage in a thorough discussion about which grade it is developmentally appropriate for students to write with a clearly defined plot—complete with a *climax*—as opposed to a beginning, middle, and end. Also, if one were to peruse some content standards that loosely define short story writing through the grade levels, students could conceivably be taught the short story almost exclusively under the narrative genre instead of experiencing other narrative forms. In these situations, it is incumbent upon teachers to interpret what type of narrative they will teach. The document designers probably did this deliberately so that teachers could have autonomy in choosing a narrative type. Even though this rationale might be valid, teachers might still feel they must delineate which type of narrative is taught and in which grade level.

In short, sometimes standards do not provide clear enough guidelines to amply assist teachers with instruction direction, so it behooves teachers to discuss expectations. These discussions are imperative, because being grounded in what is specifically taught translates to improved student writing. The clearer teachers are about the criteria of each writing genre, the better the students' work will be.

CONTINUUMS FOR OTHER SUBJECT AREAS

For those who teach subjects other than language arts, the formats and symbol keys shown in this chapter's documents can be applied to create continuums for other content areas. Teachers can use the content standards from their own state and also those from Mid-continent Research for Education and Learning (McREL), which are listed by content areas in grade-level clusters. The Web site is www.mcrel.org/standards-benchmarks/. For those unfamiliar with McREL, this quote from the organization's documentation succinctly explains their work: "McREL is well-known for its work in standards development. Its database of K–12 content standards and other valuable standards' tools are used by district- and state-level educators across the nation. McREL's Compendium, *Content Knowledge,* continues to be the most comprehensive synthesis of content standards available anywhere." Senior author John Kendall and coauthor Robert Marzano were instrumental in producing the *Content Knowledge* document, along with a host of other individuals who are acknowledged on the McREL Web site at www.mcrel.org/standards-benchmarks/docs/acknowledgment.asp.

Figure 3.2   Writing Types Continuum: Kindergarten to Eighth Grades

Writing Types Continuum: Kindergarten to Eighth Grades

This indicates what teachers expect of students in kindergarten to eighth grade in terms of writing applications or genres. In the state content standards, detailed expectations for these writing types and accompanying strategies are included.

SYMBOL KEY:

    ✱ Comprehensive unit complete with stages of the writing process

    √ Short series of lessons

    S State content standard

NARRATIVE (One narrative is expected at each grade level, although the specific type of narrative is not necessarily delineated; the chart below indicates that teachers exceed expectations of writing standard.)

	K	1st	2nd	3rd	4th	5th	6th	7th	8th
The following include a *plot*:									
Fictional short story		✱	√	✱		√		✱	√
Personal narrative		√	√	✱	√	√		✱	
The following do not include a *plot*:									
Autobiography			✱						√
Biography							✱		✱
Historical fiction				√	✱	✱		√	
Primary journal writing & class books	✱			✱					

DESCRIPTIVE (Not a state expectation for grades 4 on up; description incorporated within narrative writing.)

	K	1st	2nd	3rd	4th	5th	6th	7th	8th
Description of object, person, place, or event using sensory detail	√	✱/s	√	✱/s	√			√	√
Poetry		√		✱	√	√		✱	✱
Friendly letter			✱/s	✱	✱	√			

EXPOSITORY

	1st	2nd	3rd	4th	5th	6th	7th	8th
Formal letters			✱/s					
Thank-you notes			✱/s		√			
Invitations			✱/s					
Information reports	✱		✱	✱/s				
Research report					✱/s	✱/s	✱/s	✱/s
Summaries		√	✱	✱/s			✱/s	√
Responses to literature		✱	√	✱/s	✱/s	✱/s	✱/s	✱/s
Comparison/contrast						√		√
Problem/solution			√					
Cause/effect						√		✱
How-to			√		√			
Simple business letters			✱					✱/s
Job applications								✱/s
Technical (how-to) document								✱/s

PERSUASIVE

	1st	2nd	3rd	4th	5th	6th	7th	8th
Letter			√					
Composition			√		✱/s	✱/s	✱/s	✱/s

Copyright © 2007 by Corwin Press. All rights reserved. Reprinted from *Curriculum Mapping: A Step-by-Step Guide for Creating Curriculum Year Overviews,* by Kathy Tuchman Glass. Thousand Oaks, CA: Corwin Press, www.corwinpress.com. Reproduction authorized only for the local school site or nonprofit organization that has purchased this book.

Figure 3.3   Writing Types Continuum: Fourth to Eighth Grades

Writing Types Continuum: Fourth to Eighth Grades

This indicates what teachers expect of students in fourth to eighth grade in terms of writing applications. In the state content standards, expectations for these writing genres are detailed. The asterisk indicates that the writing type is included in the state standards; anything without an asterisk for writing types indicates that teachers go beyond state expectations (except for narrative—see note in parentheses).

SYMBOL KEY:

I: Introduction   P: Proficiency

E: Emphasis   *: State standard

NARRATIVE (one narrative is expected at each grade level, although the specific type of narrative is not necessarily delineated; the chart below indicates that teachers exceed expectations of writing standard)

	4th Grade	5th Grade	6th Grade	7th Grade	8th Grade
Autobiography		P			P
Biography			I		
Fictional (short story)	I	E	P		
Historical fiction			I	E/P	
Personal narrative	P				
Firsthand biography				E/P	

EXPOSITORY

	4th Grade	5th Grade	6th Grade	7th Grade	8th Grade
Information reports	P*				
Research report		I*	E*	E*	P*
Summaries	I*	E	P		
Responses to literature	I*	E*	E*	E*	E*
Comparison/contrast	I		P		
Cause/effect				P	
Five-paragraph essay			I*	E	P
How-to					I/E
Business letter or memorandum					I/E*
Job application					I/E*
Technical document					I/E*

DESCRIPTIVE (not a state expectation for fourth through eighth grades)

	4th Grade	5th Grade	6th Grade	7th Grade	8th Grade
Observation	I	E			
Poetry	I	E			

PERSUASIVE

	4th Grade	5th Grade	6th Grade	7th Grade	8th Grade
Persuasive letter	I				
Persuasive composition		I*	E*	E*	P*

Copyright © 2007 by Corwin Press. All rights reserved. Reprinted from *Curriculum Mapping: A Step-by-Step Guide for Creating Curriculum Year Overviews*, by Kathy Tuchman Glass. Thousand Oaks, CA: Corwin Press, www.corwinpress.com. Reproduction authorized only for the local school site or nonprofit organization that has purchased this book.

Besides McREL or state standards, teachers can refer to the following organizations for content standards to assist them in building continuums. Included in the list is contact information for language arts standards for those who want to create continuums for other strands that are not presented in the samples shown in this chapter. Teachers can search the Web for other content areas not listed here:

- National Council of Teachers of Mathematics (NCTM):
    - Phone: 703-620-9840
    - www.nctm.org/standards/

- National Science Teachers Association (NSTA):
    - Phone: 703-243-7100
    - www.nsta.org/standards

- National Center for History in the Schools (NCHS):
    - Phone: 310-825-4702
    - www.sscnet.ucla.edu/nchs/

- National Council for the Social Studies (NCSS):
    - Phone: 800-683-0812
    - www.socialstudies.org/standards/

- The National Council of Teachers of English (NCTE):
    - Phone: 217-328-3870 or 877-369-6283
    - www.ncte.org/about/over/standards/110846.htm (joint effort with NCTE and International Reading Association [IRA])

SOME FINAL THOUGHTS

Informed teachers are aware of other grade-level standards and the accompanying skills and concepts so they can teach more effectively. Grade-level teachers should not operate in isolation. A continuum provides the overarching focus, so teachers see the panoramic picture and avoid unnecessary repetition or holes in the curriculum, prepare students for learning to come, and reinforce what has already been taught. Subject-specific continuums are a vital part of the Curriculum Year Overview, because one chief purpose of creating a curriculum map is to promote articulation from grade level to grade level.

If a school or district creates, uses, or adapts a continuum featured in this chapter, allow time for the results to appear, because teachers are just beginning to use the document for articulation purposes. Students need time to catch up with clearly articulated skills. Teachers should consider the first year that the continuum is introduced a pilot year, and encourage comments along the way that can later be incorporated into a revised document. Also, I would be remiss if I did not mention the value of pre-assessment. Even if teachers create and use a continuum, they must also pre-assess students to determine individual and class levels of proficiency. Some line items included in the document might require more or less time to teach, depending upon the students' abilities. So suggest that teachers employ the tenets of differentiation when teaching to appeal to various levels of learners. As you work to revise the document, keep in mind the needs of most of the class, but realize that some students will need modifications and extensions.

Remember the metaphor mentioned in the Introduction about other menu items rather than just the balanced, basic ones of protein, starch, and vegetables. Just as chefs need to be mindful of other menu offerings besides the basics to include appetizers and desserts, so too must teachers be aware of other grade-level standards and expectations. A continuum can serve as the vehicle to clearly document and articulate these subject-specific expectations of what students should understand, know, and be able to do from one grade to the next.

4

Curriculum Year Overview Samples

Some educators teach in a self-contained or core classroom (language arts/social studies or math/science). They typically create interdisciplinary units of study to enhance learning, making connections across curricular areas as it makes sense, while others teach in a single-subject setting and cover content specific to a subject area. Single-subject teachers do not usually have the luxury of time and collegial support to intensively build a unit of study that integrates with other subjects, but there are instances in which it works well. Some single-subject teachers may operate within an interdisciplinary team so that these connections can be made for students during some units of study through content area teachers on their team. And some units of study are best served by making interdisciplinary connections as an integral part of understanding, so single-subject teachers try their best to do so in the interest of students. For example, a teacher who uses *Anne Frank: The Diary of a Young Girl* as a reading selection in a single-subject language arts class will need to tie social studies into the curriculum for students to understand the setting of the work. Without this interdisciplinary connection, students cannot fully appreciate the literature.

In this chapter, you will find Curriculum Year Overview samples for classroom teachers who teach thematic interdisciplinary units and those who focus on single-subject curriculum. Specifically, you will find samples for primary, upper elementary, middle school, and high school. Whether the sample documents are interdisciplinary-driven or single-subject, they all share these common features as explained in Chapter 2, Step #5: "Beginning the Curriculum

NOTE: Standards and benchmarks from McREL standards used in this chapter are from Marzano, Robert, and Kendall, John (2004), *Content Knowledge: A Compendium of Standards and Benchmarks for K–12 Education,* 4th ed. Aurora, CO: McREL.

Year Overview Monthly Units": (1) unit title (theme/concept and representative topic); (2) timing; (3) unit guiding questions; (4) standards; (5) skills; (6) assessments; (7) resources. Some samples include a category subtitled "Notes," which might work well for your group if you find teachers would benefit from a cursory explanation and information for a given unit.

ABOUT STANDARDS

The standards included in these sample documents are from McREL's (Mid-continent Research for Education and Learning, www.mcrel.org) *Content Knowledge: A Compendium of Standards and Benchmarks for K–12 Education* by Robert Marzano and John Kendall. McREL is widely known and respected for standards development. Their content standards appear in similar language in many state content standards, so they should resonate with all teachers. Most state standards are easily transferable, as are those from McREL, with the exception of some upper elementary social studies examples. However, participants should not be deterred from previewing the samples in this chapter simply because standards are not an identical match. There is value in perusing samples for wording of skill statements, list of resources and assessments, and unit guiding questions, as well as format.

PRIMARY

CURRICULUM YEAR

OVERVIEW EXAMPLES

PRIMARY

Curriculum Year Overview Unit Examples

The Curriculum Year Overview samples for primary grades feature a monthly sampling of interdisciplinary units for certain months only, and not the entire school year. Teachers can use these samples to see how thematic interdisciplinary units are mapped and follow this format for their own units of study. If primary teachers in your group do not teach in an interdisciplinary fashion, they might refer to the upper elementary single-subject samples. Remind participants that the CYO serves to provide an overview of what is to be taught, so these samples are meant to guide teachers when they develop their own comprehensive units. The following monthly samples are included:

- Figure 4.1: How Plants Grow and Change: Sunflowers
- Figure 4.2: Thanksgiving: Appreciation Today and Long Ago
- Figure 4.3: Fairy Tales
- Figure 4.4: The Change of Seasons
- Figure 4.5: Human Body/Senses: Getting to Know Our Bodies

In addition to mapping units, you will find routines that teachers incorporate into their daily classroom instruction. Many standards that primary teachers are expected to address are included in daily routines. They may stand alone or might be integrated within a thematic unit on a given day or week. The routines featured include standards, purpose, program overview, skills, assessments, and resources for the following daily instruction. Examples of following daily routines are included:

- Figure 4.6: Daily Routine: Calendar Time
- Figure 4.7: Daily Routine: Shared Reading
- Figure 4.8: Daily Routine: Community Circle
- Figure 4.9: Daily Routine: Read Aloud/Story Time
- Figure 4.10: Daily Routine: Journal Writing
- Figure 4.11: Daily Routine: Daily Geography
- Figure 4.12: Ongoing: Listening/Speaking

Figure 4.1   How Plants Grow and Change: Sunflowers

How Plants Grow and Change: Sunflowers

Timing: October—Grades: Primary			
Unit Guiding Questions: 1. How are plants different and alike? **2.** How do sunflowers grow and change? **3.** How do you measure the growth of a plant?			

McREL STANDARDS	SKILLS	ASSESSMENTS	RESOURCES
Science • Knows that living things go through a process of growth and change • Knows that plants need certain resources for energy and growth • Knows the basic needs of plants (e.g., air, water, nutrients, light) • Knows that there are similarities and differences in the appearance and behavior of plants • Uses the senses to make observations about living things • Records information collected about the physical world (e.g., in drawings, simple data charts) **Math** • Knows processes for measuring height using basic standard and non-standard units • Makes quantitative estimates and checks them against measurements • Collects and represents information about objects in simple graphs • Recognizes regularities in a variety of contexts (e.g., shapes) • Extends simple patterns • Understands that patterns can be made by putting different shapes together or taking them apart **Reading** • Uses mental images based on pictures and print to aid in comprehension of text • Uses reading skills and strategies to understand a variety of informational texts • Understands the main idea and supporting details of simple expository information • Summarizes information found in text (e.g., retells in own words) • Relates new information to prior knowledge **Writing** • Uses writing to describe objects • Writes for different purposes (e.g., to inform) • Uses conventions of print in writing (e.g., forms letters in print, uses upper- and lowercase letters, spaces words and sentences) • Uses complete sentences in written compositions • Uses conventions of spelling (e.g., spells high frequency words, uses letter-sound relationships) • Uses conventions of capitalization and punctuation in written compositions **Art** • Uses a variety of basic art materials to create works of art and express ideas and feelings • Experiments with a variety of textures and shapes	• Identify the differences between seeds and bulbs • Compare and sort objects by one physical attribute (e.g., color, shape, texture, size, weight) • Label major structures of common plants (e.g., stems, leaves, roots) and of a sunflower • Compare/contrast the growth of a sunflower with a bulb plant • Measure sprouts growing • Communicate observations orally and through drawings of how sprouts have grown • Compare student growth with sunflower growth • Create and extend patterns using sunflower seeds and paper petals • Estimate and verify answers to these questions: *When will the sunflower bloom? How many seeds in each flower? How long will the sunflower live?* • Comprehend and orally summarize what is read • Write with understanding of content • Write descriptively and accurately about content • Show understanding of purpose and audience • Describe sunflower and sequence of lifespan • Identify pattern of snowflakes; recreate pattern • Make collage representative of content	• Oral explanation of the difference between seeds and bulbs • Labeled drawings of plant structures • Measurements of sprouts • Journal drawings and oral explanation of sunflower's growth • Picture graph comparing student and sunflower growth • Pattern art • Estimates • Summary of information orally to include main ideas • Observation of classroom participation and discussion • Written description of sunflower; score against a rubric • Sequence of a sunflower's lifespan • Pictures emulating the style of Vincent Van Gogh • Depictions of sunflower's growth (writing and drawing) in journal • Pattern artwork • Sunflower collage	• *How a Seed Grows* by Helene J. Jordan • *From Seed to Plant* by Gail Gibbons • *Backyard Sunflower* by Elizabeth King • *The Tiny Seed* by Eric Carle • *The Seed Song* by Judy Saksie • *All About Seeds (Now I Know)* by Susan Kuchalla • *All About Seeds* by Melvin Berger • *Planting a Rainbow* by Lois Ehlert • *Sunflower House* by Eve Bunting • *Stems (Growing Flowers)* by Gail Saunders-Smith • Other nonfiction selections • "Science Stories: "New Plants" and "New Plants Module" *from* FOSS (Full Option Science System), Lawrence Hall of Science; Berkeley, CA • Sunflowers • Sunflower seeds and bulbs • Rulers • Journals • Paper petals • Math manipulatives • *The Missing Sunflowers* by Maggie Stern • *A Field of Sunflowers* by Neil Johnson • Journals • *Camille and the Sunflowers: A Story About Vincent Van Gogh* by Laurence Anholt • *Katie and the Sunflowers* by James Mayhew • Art supplies

NOTE: Standards and benchmarks are used and/or adapted by permission of McREL. Copyright © 2004, McREL.

Reprinted from *Curriculum Mapping: A Step-by-Step Guide for Creating Curriculum Year Overviews* by Kathy Tuchman Glass. Thousand Oaks, CA: Corwin Press, www.corwinpress.com. Reproduction authorized only for the local school site or nonprofit organization that has purchased this book.

Figure 4.2   Thanksgiving: Appreciation Today and Long Ago

Thanksgiving: Appreciation Today and Long Ago

Timing: November—**Grades:** Primary

Unit Guiding Questions: 1. Why is Thanksgiving a holiday? **2.** Why are you thankful? **3.** How can you show your appreciation and thanks to others? **4.** How was life long ago different and the same from life today? **5.** How have Native Americans contributed to society?

McREL STANDARDS	SKILLS/ACTIVITIES	ASSESSMENTS	RESOURCES
Social Studies • Understands the reasons that Americans celebrate certain national holidays • Knows the cultural similarities and differences in the clothes, homes, food, communication, and cul- tural traditions between families now and in the past • Understands the daily life of a colonial community • Understands the daily life and values of early Native American cultures • Understands through legends, myths the origins and culture of early Native Americans **Reading** • Uses mental images based on pictures and print to aid in comprehension of text • Uses reading skills and strategies to understand a variety of informational texts and literary works (e.g., myths and folktales) • Understands the main idea and supporting details of simple expository information • Summarizes information found in texts (e.g., retells in own words) • Relates new information to prior knowledge and experience **Writing** • Uses writing to describe persons and places • Writes for different purposes (e.g., to inform) • Uses conventions of print in writing (e.g., forms letters in print, uses upper- and lowercase letters, spaces words and sentences) • Uses complete sentences in written compositions • Uses conventions of spelling in written compositions (e.g., spells high frequency words, uses letter-sound relationships) • Uses conventions of capitalization in written compositions (e.g., first and last names, first words of a sentence) • Uses conventions of punctuation in written compositions (e.g., uses periods after declarative sentences) **Math** • Selects and uses appropriate tools for measurement situations • Understands and applies basic and advanced properties of the concept of measurement **Art** • Uses a variety of basic art materials to create works of art and express ideas and feelings	• Retell the historical origin for celebrating Thanksgiving • Brainstorm reasons for being thankful • Compare and contrast various aspects of daily and family life today versus long ago: clothing, home, food, communication, transportation, traditions • Identify similarities and differences among various Native American creation myths and folktales • List contributions Native Americans have made • Comprehend and summarize what is read • Write and draw main idea of what is learned • Identify and express in writing personal feelings • Use appropriate measuring tools • Listen and follow instructions to make butter, jam, and cornbread muffins • Weave placemats • Trace hands • Use scissors	• Venn diagram of life then and now • Story maps of characters, setting, problem/solution in myths and folktales • Observation of classroom participation and discussion Through interactive writing, teacher support, and individually, students produce the following writing: • Book with pictures and words that detail what Indians have brought to our way of life (e.g., farming methods, food, etc.) • "I Am Thankful" class book explaining what each student is thankful for • Written response to one prompt: "If I were a Pilgrim . . ." or "If I could say something to Squanto, I would say . . ." • Butter, jam, and cornbread muffins • Classroom observations • Placemats • Hand turkeys • Collage	• Various historical fiction and nonfiction for the study of Thanksgiving, Native Americans, Pilgrims • Various creation myths and folktales • Journals • Various graphic organizers • Cooking utensils and supplies • Cookbook • Art supplies • Weaving materials • Pictures of turkeys

NOTE: Standards and benchmarks are used and/or adapted by permission of McREL. Copyright © 2004, McREL.

Reprinted from *Curriculum Mapping: A Step-by-Step Guide for Creating Curriculum Year Overviews* by Kathy Tuchman Glass. Thousand Oaks, CA: Corwin Press, www.corwinpress.com. Reproduction authorized only for the local school site or nonprofit organization that has purchased this book.

Figure 4.3 Fairy Tales

Fairy Tales

Timing: December—Grades: Primary

Unit Guiding Questions: 1. How are fairy tales structured? **2.** How are fairy tales alike and different from other types of literature and from other fairy tales? **3.** Why are there different versions of the same fairy tale?

McREL STANDARDS	SKILLS/ACTIVITIES	ASSESSMENTS	RESOURCES
Reading • Uses meaning clues (e.g., picture captions, title, story structure) to aid comprehension and make predictions about content (e.g., action, events, character behavior) • Reads aloud familiar stories with fluency and expression • Uses reading skills and strategies to understand a variety of familiar literary passages • Knows the basic characteristics of familiar genres (e.g., picture books, fairy tales, nursery rhymes) • Knows setting, main characters, main events, sequence and problems in stories • Understands similarities and differences within and among literary works (e.g., fairy tales' settings, character types, events) • Knows themes that recur across literary works (fairy tales) • Summarizes information found in text (e.g., retells in own words) **Writing** • Uses the general strategies of the writing process: prewriting, drafting and revising, editing and publishing • Uses strategies to organize written work (e.g., uses a sequence of events) • Writes in [a particular] genre (i.e., fairy tale) • Uses descriptive words • Uses conventions of print in writing (e.g., forms letters in print, uses upper- and lowercase letters, spaces words and sentences, includes margins) • Uses complete sentences in written compositions • Uses conventions of spelling (e.g., spells high frequency words, uses letter-sound relationships) • Uses conventions of capitalization and punctuation in written compositions	• List eight elements of a fairy tale and identify them in literary works (e.g., begins with "Once upon a time," one character is wicked, one character is someone of royalty, etc.) • Identify the basic plot diagram ("inverted check") in fairy tales • Retell a fairy tale • Generate alternative endings to plots • Compare and contrast setting, character types, and events • Compare and contrast different versions of the same fairy tale: (*Lon Po Po* with *Little Red Riding Hood; Abuelo and the Three Bears* with *Goldilocks and the Three Bears; Yeh-Shen* with *Cinderella*) • Identify common themes in fairy tales • Read with fluency and expression • Write a fairy tale using descriptive words, sequence, complete sentences, correct grammar, and conventions • Use the writing process	• Oral explanation of the evidence of eight elements in a selected fairy tale • Story maps of characters, setting, plot in fairy tales • Venn diagram comparing and contrasting different versions of the same fairy tale • Oral reading • Observation of classroom participation and discussion Through teacher support or individually, students select and produce writing from these choices: • Fairy tale that moves through a logical sequence of events and describes the setting, characters, and events in detail **or** extension of a fairy tale **or** different version of a featured fairy tale; score against rubric	• *Rapunzel* by Bernice Chardiet • *Rumpelstiltskin* by Paul O. Zelinsky • *Hansel and Gretel* • *Lon Po Po* by Ed Young • *The True Story of the Three Little Pigs* by Jon Scieszka • *The Frog Prince Continued* by Jon Scieszka • *My Father's Dragon* (chapter book) by Ruth Stiles Gannett • *The Paper Bag Princess* by Robert Munsch • *Heckedy Peg* by Audrey and Don Wood • *The Twelve Dancing Princesses* by Marianna Mayer • *The Illustrated Book of Fairy Tales* retold by Neil Philip • See school, teacher, and public libraries for additional fairy tales • Various graphic organizers

NOTE: Standards and benchmarks are used and/or adapted by permission of McREL. Copyright © 2004, McREL.

Reprinted from Curriculum Mapping: *A Step-by-Step Guide for Creating Curriculum Year Overviews* by Kathy Tuchman Glass. Thousand Oaks, CA: Corwin Press, www.corwinpress.com. Reproduction authorized only for the local school site or nonprofit organization that has purchased this book.

Figure 4.4   The Change of Seasons

The Change of Seasons

Timing: December—Grades: Primary		
Unit Guiding Questions: **1**. Why does the weather change? **2**. How does the change in seasons affect the environment? **3**. How do icicles and crystals form? **4**. How does water evaporate?		
McREL STANDARDS	**SKILLS/ACTIVITIES**	**RESOURCES**

Science

- Knows vocabulary (e.g., rainy, windy, sunny) for different types of weather
- Knows that short-term weather conditions (e.g., temperature, rain, snow) can change daily, and weather patterns change over the seasons
- Knows how the environment changes over the seasons
- Knows that water can be a liquid or a solid and can be made to change from one form to the other, but the amount of water stays the same
- Knows that water exists in the air in different forms (e.g., in rain, snow) and changes from one form to another
- Knows that tools (e.g., thermometers) can be used to gather information and extend the senses

Math

- Collects and represents information about events on simple graphs
- Understands that patterns can be made by putting different shapes together or taking them apart

Reading

- Uses mental images based on pictures and print to aid in comprehension of text
- Uses reading skills and strategies to understand a variety of informational texts
- Understands the main idea and supporting details of simple expository information
- Summarizes information found in text
- Relates new information to prior knowledge

Writing

- Uses writing to describe people, places, and objects
- Uses descriptive words to convey basic ideas
- Uses adjectives in written composition
- Writes for different purposes (e.g., to describe)
- Use conventions of print in writing (e.g., forms letters in print, uses upper- and lowercase letters, spaces words and sentences, etc.)
- Uses complete sentences in written compositions
- Uses conventions of spelling (e.g., spells high frequency words, uses letter-sound relationships, etc.)
- Uses conventions of capitalization and punctuation

Art

- Uses a variety of basic art materials to create works of art and express ideas and feelings
- Experiments with a variety of textures and shapes

SKILLS/ACTIVITIES

- Describe how icicles and crystals are formed
- Explain the process of evaporation
- Explain how the environment changes over the seasons
- Identify different weather conditions through drawing and writing
- Read a thermometer
- Summarize reading material
- Graph weather over a period of time and draw a conclusion about results
- Use vocabulary accurately

ASSESSMENTS

- Oral explanations of how icicles and crystals form
- Journal drawings and writing (or dictation) of crystal formation and evaporation
- Weather graph with conclusions expressed through writing and drawing
- Oral summaries of reading
- Thermometer reading
- Classroom observations
- Draw expression of feelings of favorite seasons
- Identify patterns
- Create snowflakes using pattern
- Write with understanding of purpose and audience
- Write using the writing process
- Write using descriptive words to describe people, places, and objects
- Use correct grammar and punctuation
- Write complete sentences
- Use various art materials
- Drawings of favorite season
- Snowflakes with pattern

Through interactive writing, teacher support, and individually, students produce the following writing:

- Story about a snowman inspired by *Snowballs* by Lois Ehlert
- Poem about winter
- Description and drawing of favorite season and explanation about why it is the favorite season (optional: class book)

RESOURCES

- Water containers and water
- Journals
- Science kit for crystals
- Teacher-generated materials
- Science textbook
- Graphic organizers
- "Science Stories: Air and Weather" and "Air and Weather Module" *from* FOSS (Full Option Science System), Lawrence Hall of Science; Berkeley, CA
- *Rain Makes Applesauce* by Scheer and Bilbeck
- *Winter (Seasons)* by Gail Saunders-Smith
- *Autumn Leaves* by Gail Saunders-Smith
- *Sunshine (Weather)* by Gail Saunders-Smith
- *A Rainy Day (What Kind of Day Is It?)* by Lola M. Schaefer, Gail Saunders-Smith
- *Sunshine Makes the Seasons* by Franklyn M. Branley
- *Round and Round the Seasons Go* by Rozanne Lanczak Williams
- *Storms* by Susan Canizares and Betsey Chessen
- *Gilberto and the Wind* by Marie Halls Ets
- *The Wind Blew* by Pat Hutchins
- *Weather* by Pamela Chanko and Daniel Moreton
- *Snow Is Falling* by Franklyn M. Branley
- *Whatever the Weather* by Karen Wallace
- *Weather at Your Fingertips* by Judy Nayer
- *Snowballs* by Lois Ehlert
- *Once Upon Ice* by Jane Yolen
- Graphic organizers for prose and poetry
- Various picture books on seasons and weather
- *Snowballs* by Lois Ehlert
- *Snowflake Bentley* by Jacqueline Briggs Martin
- Other picture books of snowflakes
- Tissue paper
- Art supplies

NOTE: Standards and benchmarks are used and/or adapted by permission of McREL. Copyright © 2004, McREL.

Reprinted from *Curriculum Mapping: A Step-by-Step Guide for Creating Curriculum Year Overviews* by Kathy Tuchman Glass. Thousand Oaks, CA: Corwin Press. www.corwinpress.com. Reproduction authorized only for the local school site or nonprofit organization that has purchased this book.

Figure 4.5   Human Body/Senses: Getting to Know Our Bodies

Human Body/Senses: Getting to Know Our Bodies

Timing: February—**Grades:** Primary
Unit Guiding Questions: 1. How does each body part function? **2**. How are you alike and different from others? **3**. How do we use our five senses?

McREL STANDARDS	SKILLS	ASSESSMENTS	RESOURCES
Health • Knows the names and locations of some body parts • Knows the basic structure and functions of the human body systems **Science** • Uses the senses to make observations about living things • Knows that there are similarities and differences in the appearance and behavior of [humans] **Math** • Collects and represents information on simple graphs • Knows and applies processes for measuring length and weight using basic standard and non-standard units • Counts objects (e.g., toes, ribs, etc.) • Counts whole numbers • Understands basic whole number relationships • Understands the basic measures of length, height, weight **Writing** • Uses writing to describe familiar persons, places, and objects • Uses descriptive words to convey basic ideas • Uses adjectives in written composition • Writes for different purposes (e.g., to describe) • Uses conventions of print in writing (e.g., forms letters in print, uses upper- and lowercase letters, spaces words and sentences) • Uses complete sentences in written compositions • Uses conventions of spelling (e.g., spells high frequency words, uses letter-sound relationships) • Uses conventions of capitalization and punctuation in written compositions **Art** • Creates three-dimensional structures • Uses a variety of basic art materials to create works of art and express ideas and feelings **Speaking/Listening** • Recites and responds to familiar poems and rhymes with patterns	• Describe body parts and their functions • Measure and weigh self and partner • Identify human features and behaviors • Compare and contrast classmates' features (e.g., eye color, hair color and texture, etc.) and behaviors • Graph types and number of features (and behaviors) • Identify and describe each of the five senses • Conduct experiments on each of the five senses • Draw and write about observations • Write using sensory detail about people, places, and objects • Create three-dimensional skeleton out of recycled materials • Draw skeletons with accuracy • Paint self-portrait • Identify body parts • Follow directions • Count how many fingers, toes, ribs, etc., in the body • Understand "less than" and "greater than" • Compare the number of pounds (weight) and feet/inches (measurement) of adult and infant bodies	• Graphs and charts • Drawing and writing entries in journal • Descriptive writing scored against rubric • Class participation and discussion • Skeletons • Self-portrait • Observation of accurate singing and one-to-one correspondence for body parts • Journal record of math findings • Class participation and observation	• *Today I Feel Silly* by Jamie Lee Curtis • *Faces* by François and Jean Robert • *How Are You Feeling?* by Joost Elffers • *You Can't See Your Bones with Binoculars* by Harriet Ziefert • *Your Senses* (The Senses) by Helen Frost, Gail Saunders-Smith • *The Great Graph Contest* by Loreen Leedy • Objects that appeal to the five senses (e.g., vanilla extract, cotton candy, music, etc.) • Math and writing journals • Standard and non-standard measuring tools • Graphing materials • Recycled materials • Picture or model of skeletons • Art supplies • Mirrors • *Dem Bones* by Bob Barner • "Hokey Pokey" song • Measurement tools • Students • Math manipulatives

NOTE: Standards and benchmarks are used and/or adapted by permission of McREL. Copyright © 2004, McREL.

Reprinted from *Curriculum Mapping: A Step-by-Step Guide for Creating Curriculum Year Overviews* by Kathy Tuchman Glass. Thousand Oaks, CA: Corwin Press, www.corwinpress.com. Reproduction authorized only for the local school site or nonprofit organization that has purchased this book.

Figure 4.6   Daily Routine: Calendar Time

DAILY ROUTINE: Calendar Time

McREL STANDARDS:

- **Listening/Speaking:**
  - Follows rules of conversation and group discussion
  - Gives and responds to oral directions

- **Social Studies:**
  - Distinguishes among broad categories of historical time (e.g., yesterday, today, tomorrow)
  - Understands calendar time in days, weeks, and months

- **Math:**
  - Understands the concepts of time and how it is measured (e.g., calendar, day, week, month, year)
  - Knows processes for measuring temperature
  - Understands that numerals are symbols used to represent quantities or attributes (e.g., represents how many of something there is)
  - Counts whole numbers
  - Recognizes and extends simple patterns (e.g., numbers)

- **Science:**
  - Knows that tools (e.g., thermometers) can be used to gather information and extend the senses
  - Knows that short-term weather conditions can change daily, and weather patterns change over the seasons

- **Purpose**: To know the calendar system; to identify patterns
 	
- **Overview:** Each day, the teacher leads students in various cross-curricular mini-lessons involving the calendar that satisfy the skills listed below.
 	
- **Skills:**
  ○ Identify and state specific date, day of the week, month, year for today, tomorrow, and yesterday
  ○ Express the day in numerical form (i.e., 5-8-04)
  ○ Identify a specific holiday, as appropriate, and the significance of that holiday
  ○ Identify special day of any student (e.g., birthdays, lost teeth, etc.)
  ○ Recognize upcoming school events (e.g., concerts, field trips, performances, etc.)
  ○ Create, extend, and read patterns: shape, color, or number patterns
  ○ Count how many days in school thus far
  ○ Group days of school in sets
  ○ Count days of school and associate days with money value
  ○ Identify and report the day's weather; read thermometer
	- **Resources:**
	  ○ Calendar with months and days
	  ○ Sticks, coins, straws, OR base ten blocks
	  ○ Weather wheel or graph
	  ○ Thermometer
	  ○ "Today, tomorrow, yesterday" marker
	  ○ *A Day, A Week,* and *A Month* by Robin Nelson (Lerner Publications Company, Minneapolis)
	
	- **Assessments:**
	  ○ Informal observations
	  ○ Class participation and attentive listening

NOTE: Standards and benchmarks are used and/or adapted by permission of McREL. Copyright © 2004, McREL.

Reprinted from *Curriculum Mapping: A Step-by-Step Guide for Creating Curriculum Year Overviews* by Kathy Tuchman Glass. Thousand Oaks, CA: Corwin Press, www.corwinpress.com. Reproduction authorized only for the local school site or nonprofit organization that has purchased this book.

Figure 4.7   Daily Routine: Shared Reading

DAILY ROUTINE: Shared Reading

McREL READING STANDARDS:

- Uses basic elements of phonetic analysis (e.g., common letter/sound relationships, beginning and ending consonants, vowel sounds, blends, word patterns) to decode unknown words
- Uses basic elements of structural analysis (e.g., syllables, basic prefixes, suffixes, root words, compound words, spelling patterns, contractions) to decode unknown words
- Understands level-appropriate sight words and vocabulary (e.g., words for persons, places, things, actions; high frequency words such as *said, was,* and *where)*
- Uses self-correction strategies (e.g., searches for cues, identifies miscues, rereads, asks for help)
- Reads aloud familiar poems with fluency and expression (e.g., rhythm, flow, meter, tempo, pitch, tone, intonation)

- **Purpose:** To build fluency when reading aloud and comprehend what is read

- **Overview:** Through shared reading, students read and sing poems. Prior to reading, the teacher reviews words and vocabulary. Each student has a poetry binder that includes a compilation of poems read in class so they can further their expertise as readers by practicing these poems during silent reading, buddy reading, and at home. The poems change approximately every week or two; poem topics are thematically linked to subject areas and seasons.

- **Skills:**
  - Read sight words
  - Read with fluency and proper inflection
  - Become phonemically aware
  - Use context to understand word meanings
  - Respond to punctuation marks in reading
  - Understand the difference between poetry and prose
  - Recognize and recite rhyming words
  - Recognize concepts about print

- **Resources:**
  - Various poems and big books of poems
  - Poem master binder organized by month

- **Assessment:**
  - Read with accuracy and fluency
  - Identify title and author of selections
  - Classroom participation

NOTE: Standards and benchmarks are used and/or adapted by permission of McREL. Copyright © 2004, McREL.

Reprinted from *Curriculum Mapping: A Step-by-Step Guide for Creating Curriculum Year Overviews* by Kathy Tuchman Glass. Thousand Oaks, CA: Corwin Press, www.corwinpress.com. Reproduction authorized only for the local school site or nonprofit organization that has purchased this book.

Figure 4.8   Daily Routine: Community Circle

DAILY ROUTINE: Community Circle

McREL STANDARDS:

- **Social Studies (Working With Others):**
  - Demonstrates respect for others' rights, feelings, and points of view in a group
  - Uses conflict-resolution techniques
  - Actively listens to the ideas of others and asks clarifying questions
  - Uses nonverbal communication such as eye contact, body positions, and gestures effectively

- **Listening and Speaking:**
  - Makes contributions in class and group discussions
  - Asks and responds to questions
  - Follows rules of conversation and group discussion (e.g., takes turns, raises hand to speak, stays on topic, focuses on speaker)
  - Uses level-appropriate vocabulary in speech

- **Behavioral Studies:**
  - Understands that some ways of dealing with disagreements work better than others, and that people who are not involved in an argument may be helpful in solving it
  - Understands that rules at school let individuals know what to expect and so can reduce the number of disputes

---

- **Purpose:** To practice oral language skills; to respect others' opinions; to critically think about and respond to various topics

- **Overview:** Students have an opportunity to share their thoughts and opinions on certain student- and teacher-generated topics. Some topics are thematically based, and others are not. As a question is posed, students take turns responding by using a speaking stone or plastic microphone that is passed. The only student able to speak is the one holding this item. Sometimes the community circle is an opportunity to discuss classroom or playground conflicts and issues. Additionally, the community circle question can be a topic for journal writing later in the day.

- **Skills:**
  - Stand at desk erectly and face as many classmates as possible or sit with a straight back
  - Listen attentively and look at speaker
  - Speak with clarity and projection
  - Answer question with thoughtful response
  - Answer in complete sentences
  - Respect the opinions of others
  - Employ conflict-resolution techniques, as needed

- **Resources:**
  - Prepare questions, if teacher-generated
  - Speaking stone or plastic microphone
  - Jar of student-generated topics (suggestion)

- **Assessment:**
  - Class participation and attentive listening

NOTE: Standards and benchmarks are used and/or adapted by permission of McREL. Copyright © 2004, McREL.

Reprinted from *Curriculum Mapping: A Step-by-Step Guide for Creating Curriculum Year Overviews* by Kathy Tuchman Glass. Thousand Oaks, CA: Corwin Press, www.corwinpress.com. Reproduction authorized only for the local school site or nonprofit organization that has purchased this book.

Figure 4.9   Daily Routine: Read Aloud/Story Time

DAILY ROUTINE: Read Aloud/Story Time

McREL STANDARDS:

- **Reading Standards:**
  - o Uses meaning clues (e.g., title, cover, story structure) to aid comprehension and make predictions about content (e.g., action, events)
  - o Makes, confirms, and revises simple predictions about what will be found in a text
  - o Uses reading skills and strategies to understand a variety of literary passages and texts
  - o Knows setting, main characters, main events, sequence, and problem in stories
  - o Knows the main ideas or theme of a story
  - o Relates stories to personal experiences (e.g., events, characters, conflicts, themes)

- **Listening/Speaking:**
  - o Listens for a variety of purposes (i.e., for enjoyment, to learn what happened in the story)
  - o Listens to a variety of fiction
  - o Retells a story with attention to the sequence of main events
  - o Asks and responds to questions

- **Purpose:** To foster an appreciation for good literature; to model fluency and other speaking skills; to model comprehension strategies ("think aloud"); to respond to comprehension questions thoughtfully and appropriately

- **Overview:** Teachers read literature aloud as students are seated on the carpet. During reading, teachers model and ask various comprehension questions and discuss, as appropriate. Oftentimes, teachers conduct an extension activity, for example retelling, sequential order, author discussion, personal and text connections, comparison/contrast, art, or writing.

- **Skills:**
  - o Follow the sequence of the story
  - o Comprehend basic storyline
  - o Ask and answer appropriate questions
  - o Identify story elements

- **Resources:**
  - o Various picture and chapter books

- **Assessment:**
  - o Classroom participation during discussion
  - o Performance on extension activity

NOTE: Standards and benchmarks used and/or adapted by permission of McREL. Copyright © 2004, McREL.

Reprinted from *Curriculum Mapping: A Step-by-Step Guide for Creating Curriculum Year Overviews* by Kathy Tuchman Glass. Thousand Oaks, CA: Corwin Press, www.corwinpress.com. Reproduction authorized only for the local school site or nonprofit organization that has purchased this book.

Figure 4.10 Daily Routine: Journal Writing

DAILY ROUTINE: Journal Writing

McREL WRITING STANDARDS:

- Uses the general skills and strategies of the writing process: prewriting, drafting and revising, editing and publishing
- Uses strategies to organize written work (e.g., uses a sequence of events)
- Writes in a variety of forms or genres (e.g., picture books, stories, poems, personal experience narratives, responses to literature)
- Uses descriptive words to convey basic ideas
- Uses nouns, verbs, adjectives, and adverbs in written compositions
- Uses conventions of print in writing (e.g., forms letters in print, uses upper- and lowercase letters, spaces words and sentences, etc.)
- Uses complete sentences in written compositions
- Uses conventions of spelling (e.g., spells high frequency words, uses letter-sound relationships, etc.) in written compositions
- Uses conventions of capitalization and punctuation in written compositions

---

- **Purpose:** To foster an enjoyment of writing; to practice writing; to practice skills taught in teacher-directed mini-lesson; to inform teachers about instruction

- **Overview:**
  - Although all standards are covered by year's end, select specific standards appropriate for the beginning of the year and scaffold instruction.
  - On a regular basis each week, students are engaged in journal writing or writer's workshop. The topics are both student- and teacher-generated.
  - At the beginning of the year, writer's workshop will include interactive and independent writing. The ultimate goal is for all students to be independent writers, although interactive writing will be used during teacher-directed lessons to introduce new information throughout the year.
  - For formal writer's workshop, it involves a three-part format: (1) teacher-directed mini-lesson; (2) independent writing time; (3) whole class sharing (Author's Chair)
  - Students are encouraged to work at a level to which they are capable for differentiation purposes. Some will write sentences, while others are encouraged to write a paragraph or even more.
  - Students and teacher edit papers for improvement.
  - Teachers use the writing samples to inform their instruction and to show student growth.
  - Students can publish a book at the end of the year as a keepsake.

- **Skills:**
  - Write for a variety of purposes
  - Utilize appropriate organizational structure for type of writing
  - Maintain a consistent focus
  - Employ writing strategies
  - Utilize proper writing conventions and grammar
  - Use descriptive words

- **Resources:**
  - Student journals
  - *Units of Writing for Primary Writers* by Lucy Calkins (Firsthand by Heinemann, 2003)
  - *Daily Language Review, Grade 1* (Evan Moor Corp. 1998)
  - *Creating Young Writers* by Vicki Spandel and Barry Lane

- **Assessment:**
  - Written work
  - Classroom observation

NOTE: Standards and benchmarks are used and/or adapted by permission of McREL. Copyright © 2004, McREL.

Reprinted from *Curriculum Mapping: A Step-by-Step Guide for Creating Curriculum Year Overviews* by Kathy Tuchman Glass. Thousand Oaks, CA: Corwin Press, www.corwinpress.com. Reproduction authorized only for the local school site or nonprofit organization that has purchased this book.

Figure 4.11   Daily Routine: Daily Geography

DAILY ROUTINE: Daily Geography

McREL GEOGRAPHY STANDARDS:

- Understands maps can represent his or her surroundings
- Understands the globe as a representation of the earth
- Knows the basic elements of maps and globes (e.g., title, legend, cardinal directions, map symbols)

- **Purpose:** To develop an awareness of world geography by using atlases, globes, and maps; to identify where they live; to construct a simple map

- **Overview:** Every day, students will answer a series of geography questions and learn how to use geography reference materials and resources. Ultimately, students construct a simple map and identify location of home.

- **Skills:**
  - o Use geography resources to identify locations
  - o Identify elements of and specific locations on maps and globes
  - o Identify location of home
  - o Construct a simple map using cardinal directions and map symbols

- **Resources:**
  - o Student atlases
  - o Globe
  - o Classroom map
  - o *How to Make an Apple Pie and See the World* by Marjorie Priceman
  - o *Flat Stanley* by Jeff Brown
  - o *Me on the Map* by Joan Sweeney
  - o *Where Do I Live?* by Neil Chesanow
  - o *My Town* (Young Geography) by Rebecca Treays
  - o *Harcourt Brace Social Studies Daily Geography Flipbook* – teacher resource (Harcourt, Inc., 2002)

- **Assessment:**
  - o Classroom participation during discussion
  - o Accurate map
  - o Oral directions for locating home

NOTE: Standards and benchmarks are used and/or adapted by permission of McREL. Copyright © 2004, McREL.

Reprinted from *Curriculum Mapping: A Step-by-Step Guide for Creating Curriculum Year Overviews* by Kathy Tuchman Glass. Thousand Oaks, CA: Corwin Press, www.corwinpress.com. Reproduction authorized only for the local school site or nonprofit organization that has purchased this book.

Figure 4.12   Ongoing: Listening/Speaking

ONGOING: Listening/Speaking		
	McREL STANDARDS	**OVERVIEW**
POETRY	• Knows rhyming sounds and simple rhymes • Listens to a variety of poetry • Recites and responds to familiar poems and rhymes with patterns • Uses different voice level, phrasing, and intonation for different situations (e.g., presentations to class)	• Each month, students share, read, and recite poems. • Teacher uses poetry for a variety of language arts skills: listening, word detection, sound and letter recognition. • Resource: teacher-collected poems
WRITER'S WORKSHOP	• Listens for a variety of purposes (e.g., for enjoyment, to learn what happened in a story) • Uses different voice level, phrasing, and intonation for different situations (e.g., presentations to class) • Asks and responds to questions	• During journal time, students share their work (e.g., illustrations at this time of year) and classmates respond. Use these standards as a guide. • During journal or circle time, students share about personal information and events.
FOLLOWS RULES	• Follows rules of conversation and group discussion (e.g., takes turns, raises hand to speak, stays on topic, focuses attention on speaker)	• An ongoing goal during class time is to follow rules of conversation and group discussion. These skills are emphasized throughout various situations.
WEEKLY SHARING	• Uses different voice level, phrasing, and intonation for different situations (e.g., presentations to class) • Asks and responds to questions • Uses level-appropriate vocabulary in speech (e.g., words that describe people, places, things, events)	• Students participate in weekly sharing. • Topics are assigned each week and students bring in something to share that relates to the topic. • As students present their sharing, they use descriptive words and phrases to describe their object and its significance. • Option: Have students bring in their sharing hidden in a paper bag or box. Students give three clues as to the sharing object. Students guess what the object is as student reveals one clue at a time.

NOTE: Standards and benchmarks are used and/or adapted by permission of McREL. Copyright © 2004, McREL.

Reprinted from *Curriculum Mapping: A Step-by-Step Guide for Creating Curriculum Year Overviews* by Kathy Tuchman Glass. Thousand Oaks, CA: Corwin Press, www.corwinpress.com. Reproduction authorized only for the local school site or nonprofit organization that has purchased this book.

UPPER ELEMENTARY CURRICULUM YEAR OVERVIEW EXAMPLES

UPPER ELEMENTARY

Curriculum Year Overview Unit Examples

The Curriculum Year Overview samples for upper elementary grades, namely fourth and fifth grades, include a Year-at-a-Glance that shows all units in a given school year followed by various samples of detailed months for different subject areas. Both interdisciplinary and single-subject units are included.

- Figure 4.13: Year-at-a-Glance. This section shows a sample of a school's whole year mapped out. It includes representative topics and core literature to be covered in each content area month by month.
- Figure 4.14: Writing Unit: Personal Narrative. This is a formal writing lesson for a personal narrative that is scored against a rubric. It is taught early in the year for two reasons: to use as a pre-assessment tool and to learn information about students. Reading standards are included, since students are exposed to various personal narratives, both student samples and published work.
- Figure 4.15: Novel Unit: *Poppy* by Avi. This sample focuses on a core literature unit using the novel *Poppy* by Avi. Various reading standards are addressed throughout the unit. The culminating assessment is writing a short story, although students respond to literature both orally and in writing throughout the unit. Writing is scored against a rubric.
- Figure 4.16: Unit: Early Exploration of the Americas. Students study the early exploration of the Americas and culminate the unit with a PowerPoint research project and presentation both scored against student-generated criteria. This sample is interdisciplinary using social studies, language arts, and technology as the interrelated content areas.
- Figure 4.17: Unit: Mission Life-Change and Conflict. This sample is an integrated social studies and language arts unit. Students study the changes and conflicts before, during, and after the mission period and write a research report demonstrating evidence of social studies and language arts concepts, skills, and strategies.
- Figure 4.18: Unit: Rocks and Minerals in Our Ever-Changing Planet. This is a sample map of a science unit, in which students explore two principles: (1) the three types of rocks (i.e., igneous, sedimentary, and metamorphic) are classified according to specific properties; (2) the earth's surface is shaped and reshaped by slow and fast processes.
- Figure 4.19: Unit: Fractions, Mixed Numbers. This math sample shows a curriculum overview for a fractions and mixed numbers unit.

Figure 4.13 Year-at-a-Glance

Year-at-a-Glance

	Social Studies	Literature	Writing [Presentations]	Grammar	Science	Math
September	U.S. Geography Pre-Columbian settlements in North America	• *Holes* by Louis Sachar <u>or</u> *Mrs. Frisby and the Rats of NIMH* by Robert C. O'Brien • Various Native American myths and legends [narrative] [Native American]	• District Pre-Assessment (first week of school) • Narrative	• Sentence fragments/run-ons • Dialogue tags • Quotation marks for dialogue • Ongoing spelling program throughout the year	Investigation and Experimentation	• Math Pre-Assessment • Rectangle Arrays • Factors Number • Prime & Composite Numbers • Square Numbers • Factor Strings & Prime Factorization • Addition & Subtraction of Whole Numbers & Decimals
October	Early Exploration of the Americas	*Sign of the Beaver* by Elizabeth George Speare <u>or</u> *Stowaway* by Karen Hess (historical fiction)	• District Writing Prompt #1 (October) • Explorer Research Report [Explorer reports]	• Quotation marks for quoting words directly from source • Bibliography format • Review of basic capitalization rules		• Estimation • Multiplication of Whole Numbers and Decimals • Comparing Millions, Billions, and Trillions • Angle Measures • Congruent Triangles • Properties of Polygons • Tessellations
November			Response to Literature	• Compound sentences • Complex sentences • Coordinating and subordinating conjunctions • Dependent clauses • Independent clauses	Physical Sciences: Matter	• Angles of Polygons • Partial-Quotient Division Algorithm • Division of Decimals • Fraction Review • Mixed Numbers • Ordering of Fractions
December	Colonial Settlements: conflict and cooperation with other nations and Indians, key figures, slavery, religion, colonies, politics	*The Witch of Blackbird Pond* by Elizabeth George Speare (historical fiction)		• Transitions • Adverbs as modifiers • Punctuating/capitalizing titles		• Equivalent Fractions • Fractions & Decimals • Convert Fractions to Percents • Bar & Circle Graphs

(Continued)

Figure 4.13 (Continued)

86

	Social Studies	Literature	Writing [Presentations]	Grammar	Science	Math
January	Colonial settlements: conflict and cooperation with other nations and Indians, key figures, slavery, religion, colonies, politics (cont'd. from Dec.)	*The Witch of Blackbird Pond* (**cont'd.**)	• Colonial Research Report • District Prompt #2 (February) [Colonial Fair]	• Verbs: often misused • Adjectives • Commas to separate adjectives • Pronouns • Colons to introduce list	Physical Sciences: Matter (cont'd.)	• Organizing Data • Analysis of Sample Data • Common Denominators • Exponential Notation • Scientific Notation • Order of Operations • Mid-Year Assessment
February	American Revolution: causes, major battles, leaders, roles of other nations, Continental Congress, roles of women, Declaration of Independence	*My Brother Sam Is Dead* by Collier and Collier (historical fiction)		• Bibliography format (review)	Earth Sciences: Weather and Solar System	• Adding & Subtracting Negative Numbers • Adding & Subtracting Mixed Numbers • Area Model for Fraction Multiplication • Multiplication of Fractions • Percentages • District MAC Assessment
March			• Biographies • Response to Literature • Persuasive [American Revolution]	• Participles • Sentence fragments/run-ons (review) • Dialogue punctuation (review)		• Division of Fractions • Coordinate Graphs • Area of Triangles, Parallelograms, & Circles • Volume of Prism • Capacity
April	• U.S. Constitution and democracy • Waves of European immigration, 1789–1850	*Phantom Tollbooth* by Norman Jester *or* *Mrs. Frisby and the Rats of NIMH* by Robert C. O'Brien	Narrative [Government]	Appositives and commas Prepositions Prepositional phrases Parentheses	Life Sciences: Plants and Animals	• Pan-Balance Problems • Algebraic Expressions • Rates with Formulas, Tables, & Graphs • Reading Graphs • Circumference of a Circle • Review of Geometric Solids
May	• States and Territories up to 1850 • Exploration west of the Mississippi River • Westward Movement • Location of 50 states and names of their capitals	Teacher read-aloud or literature circles	• State Research Report • District Prompt #3 (May) [Westward Simulation] [State Reports]			• Volume of Cylinders, Pyramids, & Cones • Capacity & Weight • Surface Area • Factor Trees • Ratios of Parts to Wholes • Number Models for Ratio Number Stories
June						• Collecting, Graphing, & Interpreting Data • End-of-the-Year Assessment

Copyright © 2007 by Corwin Press. All rights reserved. Reprinted from *Curriculum Mapping: A Step-by-Step Guide for Creating Curriculum Year Overviews*, by Kathy Tuchman Glass. Thousand Oaks, CA: Corwin Press. www.corwinpress.com. Reproduction authorized only for the local school site or nonprofit organization that has purchased this book.

Figure 4.14 Writing: Personal Narrative

WRITING UNIT: Personal Narative—**TIMING:** September to October

Unit Guiding Questions: 1. How does the structure of a personal narrative compare with other forms of writing? **2.** Why do people write personal narratives? **3.** How do writers create compelling personal narratives?

NOTES	ASSESSMENTS	RESOURCES
• As the year begins, students write a personal narrative. • This writing is used for teachers to pre-assess students' writing abilities and to learn more about students. • The topic can be teacher-generated. Options: write about your best or worst day, write about a summer experience, write about what you hope to learn this year, write about how you learn best for success, write about a memorable family experience, etc. • The topic can also be student-generated; students can brainstorm a list of options for a topic and then choose one.	• Teacher observation of student participation in whole class and small group tasks and discussions • Graphic organizer • Student journals (respond to personal narratives) • Note taking and quizzes on writing strategies and skills • Personal narrative scored against genre-based rubric	• *Open Court* textbook and supplemental materials • Student and published samples of personal narratives • *Houghton Mifflin, English* textbook (Houghton Mifflin) • *WriteTraits Student Traitbook* and *WriteTraits Teacher's Guide* (Great Source Education Group) • *Writers Express* (Great Source Education Group) • *Creating Writers Through 6-Trait Writing Assessment and Instruction* (4th Edition) by Vicki Spandel • *6+1 Traits of Writing* by Ruth Culham • Thesaurus and dictionary • Various graphic organizers • Teacher-compiled materials

McREL STANDARDS/SKILLS

Writing	Reading
• **Writes autobiographical compositions** (e.g., provides a context within which the incident occurs, uses simple narrative strategies, and provides some insight into why this incident is memorable) • Uses the general strategies of the **writing process:** prewriting, drafting and revising, editing and publishing • Uses strategies to write for different **audiences** • Uses strategies to write for a variety of **purposes** • Uses **descriptive language** that clarifies and enhances ideas (e.g., sensory details) • Uses **paragraph form** in writing • Uses a variety of **sentence structures** in writing • Uses **pronouns, verbs,** and **nouns** in written compositions • Uses conventions of **spelling, capitalization,** and **punctuation** in written compositions	• Establishes a **purpose for reading** (e.g., to understand a specific viewpoint) • Makes, confirms, and revises simple **predictions** about what will be found in a text • Understands the **author's purpose** • Uses **reading skills and strategies** to understand a variety of literary passages and texts • States and recognizes the **defining characteristics** of a variety of literary forms and genres • Identifies **similarities and differences** within and among literary works from various genres

NOTE: Standards and benchmarks are used and/or adapted by permission of McREL. Copyright © 2004, McREL.

Reprinted from *Curriculum Mapping: A Step-by-Step Guide for Creating Curriculum Year Overviews* by Kathy Tuchman Glass. Thousand Oaks, CA: Corwin Press, www.corwinpress.com. Reproduction authorized only for the local school site or nonprofit organization that has purchased this book.

Figure 4.15   Novel Unit: *Poppy* by Avi

NOVEL UNIT: *Poppy* by Avi—**TIMING:** September to October

Unit Guiding Questions: 1. Why is setting important to the story? **2.** How do the characters change throughout the story? **3.** How does the author create suspense? **4.** How does the use of figurative language affect the story? **5.** How does this allegory compare with life?

SKILLS/ACTIVITIES	ASSESSMENTS	RESOURCES
• Define elements of literature and identify how they interrelate in reading selections (i.e., plot, setting, character, point of view, theme) • Write short story incorporating elements of literature • Write responses to literature (i.e., formal and informal; written and oral) • Write natural dialogue modeled after characters • Use correct dialogue punctuation • Indent paragraphs • Use a variety of sentence structures • Use the writing process • Identify and write with audience and purpose in mind • Use descriptive language (i.e., sensory details, strong word choice) • Use proper grammar and conventions in writing • Make, confirm, revise predictions • Use reading strategies: pause, reread, consult another source, draw upon background knowledge, ask for help • Use context clues to decode unknown words	• Teacher observation • Classroom participation in whole class and small group discussions • Sensory detail chart (setting) • Various vocabulary activities (ongoing) • Dialogue writing assignment • Character motivation and transformation assignment • Dialectical journal with responses to literature • Note taking • Graphic organizer • Culminating assessment: narrative scored against a rubric	• *Poppy* by Avi • *Poppy* literature unit (see Kathy Glass's unit) • Dialectical journal • Teacher-compiled and generated materials • Graphic organizers • Dictionary and thesaurus

McREL STANDARDS	
Writing • **Writes narrative accounts,** such as **stories** (e.g., develops characters, setting, and plot; creates an organizing structure; sequences events; uses concrete sensory details; uses strategies such as dialogue) • **Writes in response to literature** (e.g., summarizes main ideas and significant details; relates own ideas to supporting details; advances and supports judgments) • Uses the general strategies of the **writing process:** prewriting, drafting and revising, editing and publishing • Uses strategies to write for different **audiences** and a variety of **purposes** • Uses **descriptive language** that clarifies and enhances ideas (e.g., sensory details) • Uses **paragraph form** in writing • Uses a variety of **sentence structures** in writing • Uses **adjectives, verbs,** and **nouns** in written compositions • Uses conventions of **spelling, capitalization,** and **punctuation** in written compositions	**Reading** • Establishes a **purpose for reading** (e.g., to understand a specific viewpoint) • Uses a variety of **context clues** to decode unknown words • Makes, confirms, and revises simple **predictions** about what will be found in a text • Uses **reading skills and strategies** to understand a variety of literary passages and texts • Knows the **defining characteristics** of a variety of literary forms and genres • Understands the basic concept of **plot** • Understands **similarities and differences** within and among literary works from various genres • Understands elements of **character development** in literary works • Knows **themes** that recur across literary works • Understands the ways in which **language** is used in literary texts

NOTE: Standards and benchmarks are used and/or adapted by permission of McREL. Copyright © 2004, McREL.

Reprinted from *Curriculum Mapping: A Step-by-Step Guide for Creating Curriculum Year Overviews* by Kathy Tuchman Glass. Thousand Oaks, CA: Corwin Press, www.corwinpress.com. Reproduction authorized only for the local school site or nonprofit organization that has purchased this book.

Figure 4.16   Unit: Early Exploration of the Americas

UNIT: Early Exploration of the Americas—TIMING: Mid-October to November

Unit Guiding Questions: 1. Why did Europeans choose to explore and colonize the world? **2.** What were the routes and distances traveled of the major land explorers of the United States? **3.** How did fears and superstitions of the times affect exploration? **4.** How did explorers, sponsors, and leaders of key European expeditions overcome obstacles and accomplish their goals? **5.** How did sailors react when they reached their destinations?

SKILLS/ACTIVITIES	ASSESSMENTS	RESOURCES
• Brainstorm and confirm technology early explorers used • Trace the routes and distances traveled of early explorers • Name key European expeditions • Identify the aims, obstacles, accomplishments of explorers, sponsors, leaders of key European expeditions • Locate on N. and S. American maps the land claimed by European countries • Explain why Europeans chose to explore and colonize • Design, develop, publish, present PowerPoint research presentation • Frame questions that direct PowerPoint research investigation • Establish a controlling topic and develop topic with facts, details, examples, explanations • Present PowerPoint project to the class using inflection/modulation of voice, tempo, volume, enunciation, eye contact, posture • Write from the point of view of an explorer, sponsor, or leader	• Teacher observation of participation in whole class and small group tasks and discussions • Note taking • Historical journal from perspective of explorer, sponsor, or leader • Chart of land claimed • Note taking during PowerPoint presentations • "Five Reasons for Exploration" mini-book • Objective and essay test • Explorer research PowerPoint project and presentation scored against a rubric	• Various resources and different textbooks for differentiation purposes • Selected lessons from Teacher's Curriculum Institute (TCI) *History Alive! America's Past* curriculum binders; videos • *American Will Be* (Houghton Mifflin, 1991) textbook as resource • *The First Americans* textbook for Pre-Columbians by Joy Hakim • Maps and globes • Computers, dictionary, thesaurus

McREL STANDARDS	
Writing • Writes expository compositions (e.g., identifies and stays on topic; develops the topic with simple facts, details, examples, explanations; excludes extraneous and inappropriate information; uses structures such as cause-and-effect, chronology; uses several sources of information; provides a concluding statement) • Writes expressive compositions (e.g., expresses ideas, reflections, and observations; uses an individual, authentic voice; uses narrative strategies, relevant details, and ideas that enable the reader to imagine the world of the event or experience) **History** • Knows the features of the major European explorations that took place between the 15th and 17th centuries (e.g., routes and motives of	Spanish, Dutch, and English explorers; the goals and achievements of major expeditions; problems encountered on the high seas; fears and superstitions of the times; what sailors expected to find when they reached their destinations) **Technology** • Knows the characteristics and uses of **computer software programs** **Listening/Speaking** • Makes basic **oral presentations** to class • Uses a variety of verbal **communication skills** • **Organizes ideas** for oral presentations

NOTE: Standards and benchmarks are used and/or adapted by permission of McREL. Copyright © 2004, McREL.

Reprinted from *Curriculum Mapping: A Step-by-Step Guide for Creating Curriculum Year Overviews* by Kathy Tuchman Glass. Thousand Oaks, CA: Corwin Press, www.corwinpress.com. Reproduction authorized only for the local school site or nonprofit organization that has purchased this book.

Figure 4.17 Unit: Mission Life/Change and Conflict

Unit: Mission Life/Change and Conflict—**Timing:** November/December

Unit Guiding Questions: 1. How did the Spanish colonize California? **2.** How did the soldiers, missionaries, and Indians interact with one another? **3.** How did Spain's strategy for locating missions benefit them and their religious beliefs? **4.** How was daily life different between native and nonnative peoples? **5.** How did the Franciscans affect the Native Californians' culture and way of life? 6. How did the Mexican War for Independence affect Alta California?

SKILLS		ASSESSMENTS
Social Studies: • Describe how Spain colonized California • Analyze the hierarchical relationships between the soldiers, missionaries, and natives • Describe the process by which Spain chose mission sites • Compare and contrast the lives of Native Californians prior to and during the mission period • Outline the jobs of each person at the mission (soldiers, missionaries, and Native Californians) • Cite references used in information report • Discuss and describe the different vantage points associated with the Mexican War for Independence; describe the effect on Alta California, including economic gains	**Reading/Writing:** • Use reading skills and strategies (e.g., rereading, clarifying, summarizing) • Use text organizers • Write multiple-paragraph information report • Use writing process strategies • Write using various sentence structures • Use transitional devices • Employ grammar and mechanics of writing • Quote and paraphrase information from a variety of sources • Gather and use information for research: plan research, use multiple resources, record information, compile information, cite sources	• Teacher observation • Classroom discussion • Writing process evidence: notetaking, outlining, drafts, etc. • Written research report scored against a rubric that demonstrates evidence of language arts and social studies skills and strategies
		RESOURCES
		• *Harcourt Brace Social Studies: California* (2000), Chapter 3: "Spanish California," pages 142–161; Chapter 4: "Mexican California" • *Houghton Mifflin, English* textbook (Houghton Mifflin) • *Writers Express* (Great Source Education Group) • Differentiated primary and secondary source materials including Web sites

McREL STANDARDS	
History Understands the **people, events, problems, and ideas that were significant in creating the history of their state** • Understands geographic, economic, and religious reasons that brought the first explorers and settlers to the state or region, who they were, and where they settled • Understands patterns and changes in population over time • Knows the chronological order of major historical events that are part of the state's history, their significance and the impact on people then and now, and their relationship to the history of the nation • Understands major historical events and developments in the state or region that involved interaction among various groups • Understands how the ideas of significant people affected the history of the state • Understands the unique historical conditions that influenced the formation of the state and how statehood was granted	**Reading** • Uses **reading skills and strategies** to understand a variety of information texts • Uses **text organizers** to determine the main ideas and to locate information in a text • Understands **structural organization in information texts** **Writing** • Writes **expository composition** (e.g., identifies and stays on topic; develops the topic with simple facts, details, examples, and explanations; uses several sources of information; provides a conclusion) • Uses the general strategies of the writing process: prewriting, drafting and revising, editing and publishing • Uses stylistic and rhetorical aspects of writing: Uses **paragraph** form in writing, a **variety of sentence structures, transitional** devices • Uses **grammar** and the **conventions** of spelling, punctuation, and capitalization • **Gathers and uses information for research purposes**: uses a variety of strategies to plan research; uses multiple resources to gather information; uses strategies to gather and record information; uses strategies to compile information into written reports; cites information sources

NOTE: Standards and benchmarks are used and/or adapted by permission of McREL. Copyright © 2004, McREL.

Reprinted from *Curriculum Mapping: A Step-by-Step Guide for Creating Curriculum Year Overviews* by Kathy Tuchman Glass. Thousand Oaks, CA: Corwin Press, www.corwinpress.com. Reproduction authorized only for the local school site or nonprofit organization that has purchased this book.

Figure 4.18   Unit: Rocks and Minerals in Our Ever-Changing Planet

---

UNIT: Rocks and Minerals in Our Ever-Changing Planet—**TIMING:** Fall

Unit Guiding Questions: 1. How do we identify rocks and minerals? **2.** How are rocks formed? **3.** How is the Earth's surface shaped and reshaped? **4.** How is our area affected by changes of the Earth's surface?

SKILLS	ASSESSMENTS	RESOURCES
• Define properties of rocks and minerals • Test for the presence of minerals in rocks • Compare and contrast the formation of rocks • Identify and define the slow and fast processes of the Earth's changing surface • Write using personification	• Pre-assessment • Teacher observation of participation in whole class and small group tasks and discussion • Homework • Journal responses • Recorded observations and notetaking • Personification writing assignment • Culminating assessment: unit exam that includes objective and essay responses; unit guiding questions included in assessment	• "Earth Materials" FOSS Kit (Lawrence Hall of Science, Berkeley, CA) • FOSS Kit student journals • Handouts, homework sheets, and overheads from FOSS Kit • Rock samples • Pictures, videoclips, and sound bites of earth's natural processes (earthquakes, landslides, erosion, etc.) • Various articles and textbook excerpts of causes/effects of natural processes • "Rocks and Minerals" unit (Johnna Becker's unit)

McREL STANDARDS/SKILLS

- Knows how features on the Earth's surface are constantly changed by a combination of slow and rapid processes (e.g., slow processes, such as weathering, erosion, transport, and deposition of sediment caused by waves, wind, water, and ice; rapid processes, such as landslides, volcanic eruptions, and earthquakes)

- Knows that smaller rocks come from the breakage and weathering of larger rocks and bedrock

- Knows that rock is composed of different combinations of minerals

- Knows processes involved in the rock cycle (e.g., old rocks at the surface gradually weather and form sediments that are buried, then compacted, heated, and often recrystallized into new rock; this new rock is eventually brought to the surface by the forces that drive plate motions, and the rock cycle continues)

- Knows that sedimentary, igneous, and metamorphic rocks contain evidence of the minerals, temperatures, and forces that created them

---

NOTE: Standards and benchmarks are used and/or adapted by permission of McREL. Copyright © 2004, McREL.

Reprinted from Curriculum Mapping: A Step-by-Step Guide for Creating Curriculum Year Overviews by Kathy Tuchman Glass. Thousand Oaks, CA: Corwin Press, www.corwinpress.com. Reproduction authorized only for the local school site or nonprofit organization that has purchased this book.

Figure 4.19   Unit: Fractions, Mixed Numbers

UNIT: Fractions, Mixed Numbers—TIMING: February			
Unit Guiding Questions: 1. How can a whole be divided into equal parts? **2.** How can fractions and whole numbers be expressed in different ways? **3.** How can we add and subtract different fractions and mixed numbers? **4.** How are division and fractions related? **5.** How do I use fractions and mixed numbers in my life? **6.** How do people use fractions and mixed numbers in the world?			
McREL STANDARDS	**SKILLS**	**ASSESSMENTS**	**RESOURCES**
• Understands the relative magnitude and relationships among whole numbers, fractions, and mixed numbers • Adds and subtracts simple fractions • Uses models (e.g., number lines) to identify, order, and compare numbers • Uses a variety of strategies to understand problem situations (e.g., modeling problem with diagrams or physical objects)	• Write a fraction for a part of a region or a part of a group (Lessons 7.1, 7.2) • Find the fractional part of a number (7.1, 7.2) • Identify fractions that name the same number (7.3, 7.4) • Find equivalent fractions (7.3, 7.4) • Identify simplest form (7.3, 7.4) • Compare and order fractions with like or unlike denominators (7.6) • Write equivalent improper fractions and mixed numbers (7.7) • Add and subtract fractions and mixed numbers with like denominators (7.9, 7.10) • Use fractions to solve problems (7.11)	• Pre-Assessment • Homework • Quizzes • Observation of small and whole group participation • "Fractions" mini-book • Various differentiated projects • Post-test	• *Houghton Mifflin Mathematics, Level 4, Volume 1* (copyright 2002), Chapter 7: "Fractions and Mixed Numbers" • Pizza, apple • Manipulatives • Picture books with fraction theme

NOTE: Standards and benchmarks are used and/or adapted by permission of McREL. Copyright © 2004, McREL.

Reprinted from *Curriculum Mapping: A Step-by-Step Guide for Creating Curriculum Year Overviews* by Kathy Tuchman Glass. Thousand Oaks, CA: Corwin Press, www.corwinpress.com. Reproduction authorized only for the local school site or nonprofit organization that has purchased this book.

MIDDLE SCHOOL CURRICULUM YEAR OVERVIEW EXAMPLES

MIDDLE SCHOOL

Curriculum Year Overview Unit Examples

The middle school samples include a Year-at-a-Glance (Figure 4.20) and units of instruction for November/December (Figures 4.21 & 4.22) for a core teacher who integrated language arts and social studies. Additionally, you will find a short story unit for a single-subject language arts teacher entitled "The Structure and Impact of the Short Story" (Figure 4.23).

Figure 4.20 Year-at-a-Glance

	Social Studies	Literature	Writing [Presentations]	Conventions	Science
September	CHANGE/CONTINUITY • Colonial America • Great Awakening • Causes of the Revolution • Declaration of Independence • American Revolution	• Short stories (fiction) • Historical novel choices: *The Fighting Ground* by Avi; *My Brother Sam Is Dead* by Collier; *April Morning* by Fast	• Short Story • Autobiography • Response to Literature [students recite a section of the Declaration of Independence]	• <u>Sentence structures</u> (types): compound, complex, etc. • <u>Sentence openings</u> • Grammar • Punctuation • Capitalization • Spelling	MOTION • Velocity • Average Speed • Interpreting Graphs
October	GOVERNMENT SYSTEMS • Documents • U.S. Constitution • Articles of Confederation • Major debates and political philosophy	*Johnny Tremain* by Esther Forbes	• Short Story • Response to Literature [students recite the "Preamble"]		FORCES • Balanced and Unbalanced Forces • Gravity
November	GOVERNMENT SYSTEMS • State constitutions • Ordinances • Political parties • Domestic resistance • Political process • Free press	• "Harrison Bergeron" • *The Giver* by Lois Lowry	• Response to Literature • Persuasive [Amendment project presented to the class]	• <u>Parallelism</u> • Grammar • Punctuation • Capitalization • Spelling	STRUCTURE OF MATTER • Structure of Atoms • Compounds • Electrons
December	CULTURES • People of the new nation • Capitalism FOREIGN POLICY • War of 1812 • Monroe Doctrine • American Indian treaties		• Persuasive (cont'd.) • Response to Literature [Proposed bill presented to the class]		• Solids, Liquids, Gasses

(Continued)

Figure 4.20 (Continued)

	Social Studies	Literature	Writing [Presentations]	Conventions	Science
January	REFORM	Poetry	• Poetry • Response to Literature [poem presented to class]	• Apposition • Grammar • Punctuation • Capitalization • Spelling	• Periodic Table • Isotopes
February	STRIVING FOR INDEPENDENCE • Abolitionists • Northwest Ordinance • Compromise of 1850 • States' Rights Doctrine • Missouri Compromise • Free blacks	*Flowers for Algernon* by Daniel Keyes	• Research Report • Response to Literature	• Grammar • Punctuation • Capitalization • Spelling • Bibliography	CHEMICAL REACTIONS
March	CONFLICT/ COOPERATION • Causes of the Civil War • Civil War	• Civil War literature circles (differentiated list): • *With Every Drop of Blood* by James and Christopher Collier • *Killer Angels* by Michael Shaara • *Amelia's War* by Ann Rinaldi • *No Man's Land* by Susan Bartoletti • *Bull Run* by Paul Fleischman • *Abraham's Battle* by Sara Banks • *Soldier's Heart* by Gary Paulsen • *Voices of the Civil War* by Richard Wheeler • *A Photobiography of Abraham Lincoln* by Russell Freedman			CHEMISTRY OF LIVING THINGS • Carbon and Its Role • Living Organisms
April			• Documents related to career development • Response to Literature	• Grammar • Punctuation • Capitalization • Spelling	• DENSITY • BUOYANCY
June/May	ECONOMIC TRANSFORMATION	*The Pearl* by John Steinbeck		Review of all skills	EARTH IN THE SOLAR SYSTEM • Galaxies • Stars • Solar System

Figure 4.21 Unit: Revolution and a New Nation

UNIT: Revolution and a New Nation—TIMING: November/December

History Unit Guiding Questions: 1. How did certain events contribute to the American Revolution? **2.** How did key individuals become the leaders of the American Revolutionary time period? **3.** How did the colonists win the war? **4.** How did the ideals of the American Revolution influence various groups of people during and after the war?

Reading Unit Guiding Questions: 1. Why are text features important? **2.** Why is it beneficial to know the organizational structure of text? **3.** How are notes and outlines formatted to best represent text? **4.** How do we read critically for various purposes?

NOTES/SKILLS	ASSESSMENTS	RESOURCES

• During this integrated social studies and language arts unit, students read a variety of informational text and historical fiction related to the American Revolutionary time period.
 	
• Use the guiding questions continuously to set the stage for the unit, as a pre-assessment, during instruction, and for a post-assessment.
 	
• Teach and practice these reading skills and strategies to assist students in comprehending and analyzing text presented.
 	
  o Use reading strategies: pause, reread, consult another source, draw upon background knowledge, ask for help
  o Identify the structural organization of informational text
  o Use text organizers
  o Summarize and paraphrase information
  o Draw conclusions and make inferences based on explicit and implicit information
  o Compare/contrast and confirm/deny information found in various sources (historical fiction and informational texts)
	• Participation during small group and class discussion and simulations
	
	• Teacher's Curriculum Institute (TCI) notebooks
	
	• Cornell Notes or other notetaking formats
	
	• Oral participation in small group and class discussion
	
	• Reading journals
	
	• Objective and essay test
	
	• Readiness-based differentiated projects
	
	• Unit guiding questions: pre- and post-assessments
		• Various resources and different textbooks for differentiation purposes; Teacher's Curriculum Institute (TCI) curriculum binders; videos.
		
		• Textbook: *The Prentice Hall American Nation* (2000)
		
		• *Content Area Reader: The United States Change and Challenge* (Holt, Rinehart, Winston), selections from Chapters 1 and 2
		
		• Historical fiction: *The Fighting Ground* by Avi; *My Brother Sam Is Dead* by Collier; *April Morning* by Fast; *Johnny Tremain* by Forbes; "Paul Revere's Ride" by Henry Wadsworth Longfellow

McREL STANDARDS

History	Reading
• Understands the **causes of the American Revolution,** the ideas and interests involved in shaping the revolutionary movement, and reasons for the American victory (e.g., strategic elements of the Revolutionary War; impact of European countries and individual Europeans on victory; creation of the Declaration of Independence, etc.) • Understands the **impact of the American Revolution** on politics, economy, and society (e.g., political and economic issues addressed by the Continental Congress; how the ideals of the American Revolution influenced the goals of various groups during and after the war)	• Uses specific strategies to **clear up confusing parts of a text** • Uses **reading skills and strategies** to understand a variety of literary passages and informational texts • Knows the defining **characteristics of historical fiction and informational texts** • **Summarizes and paraphrase** information in texts • **Draws conclusions** and **makes inferences** based on explicit and implicit information in texts • **Defines elements of literature** in historical fiction; discern fact from fiction • **Makes connections between historical fiction and information sources**

NOTE: Standards and benchmarks are used and/or adapted by permission of McREL. Copyright © 2004, McREL.

Copyright © 2007 by Corwin Press. All rights reserved. Reprinted from *Curriculum Mapping: A Step-by-Step Guide for Creating Curriculum Year Overviews*, by Kathy Tuchman Glass. Thousand Oaks, CA: Corwin Press, www.corwinpress.com. Reproduction authorized only for the local school site or nonprofit organization that has purchased this book.

Figure 4.22 Unit: Research Report About Revolution and a New Nation

UNIT: Research Report About Revolution and a New Nation—**TIMING:** November/December			

Guiding Questions: 1. How is research writing similar and different from other genres? **2.** How is a research paper organized? **3.** How does research writing benefit readers? **4.** How can you write an informative research paper? **5.** How do you find resources to use for your research paper?

NOTES	SKILLS	ASSESSMENTS	RESOURCES
• During the integrated social studies and language arts unit, students write a research paper based on a topic of their choice from the social studies content. • Students present the highlights of their research findings to the class along with visual aids. • Introduce and continuously refer to the guiding questions during instruction. • Use reading strategies (see "Revolution and a New Nation") in addition to the writing and listening/speaking skills and standards to guide instruction.	**Research Writing:** • State thesis • Write information that reflects knowledge about report topic • Organize information in a logical manner • Include introduction, body paragraphs, and conclusion • Use own words to develop ideas • Use accurate terms • Use expository structures and features • Employ the writing process • Be clear about audience and purpose **Presenting:** • Use notes and organizational pattern when presenting • Use visual aids in presentation • Use appropriate verbal and nonverbal techniques (e.g., inflection/modulation of voice, tempo, enunciation, physical gestures, eye contact, posture) • Evaluate own and others' presentations against criteria	• Observations • Writing process pieces: graphic organizers (webs, outlines), notes, drafts, and so on • Research paper scored against a standards-based rubric • Presentation scored against a standards-based rubric	• Various primary and secondary resources • Textbook: *The Prentice Hall American Nation* (2000) and other textbook excerpts • Published and student writing samples • *Colonial Life and the American Revolution* (Teacher's Curriculum Institute): "Journal," (Section 1); "Editorial," (Section 3) • *Inside Writing* (Great Source Education Group)

McREL STANDARDS	

Writing

• Writes research paper
• Uses the general skills and strategies of the writing process: prewriting, drafting and revising, editing and publishing
• Uses content, style, and structure appropriate for specific audiences and purposes
• Uses library catalogs and databases to locate sources for research topics
• Uses a variety of resource materials to gather information for research topics

• Determines the appropriateness of an information source for a research topic
• Organizes information and ideas from multiple sources in systematic ways
• Uses appropriate methods to cite and document reference sources

Listening/Speaking

• Makes formal presentations to the class
• Uses appropriate verbal and nonverbal techniques for oral presentations
• Responds to questions and feedback about own presentations
• Uses criteria to evaluate others' effectiveness in formal presentations

NOTE: Standards and benchmarks are used and/or adapted by permission of McREL. Copyright © 2004, McREL.

Reprinted from *Curriculum Mapping: A Step-by-Step Guide for Creating Curriculum Year Overviews* by Kathy Tuchman Glass. Thousand Oaks, CA: Corwin Press, www.corwinpress.com. Reproduction authorized only for the local school site or nonprofit organization that has purchased this book.

Figure 4.23 Unit: The Structure and Impact of the Short Story

UNIT: The Structure and Impact of the Short Story—**TIMING:** January		
Guiding Questions: 1. How does the structure of a short story compare with other forms of writing? **2.** How do the elements of literature interrelate in specific short stories? **3.** How do the qualities of some stories make them ageless and enjoyable for all readers? **4.** How do writers create compelling short stories?		
SKILLS	**ASSESSMENTS**	**RESOURCES**

• Define and analyze five elements of literature: *plot, setting, point of view, character, theme*
• Identify elements of literature in various short stories
• Compare and contrast settings, points of view, characters, plot, and theme across various short story selections
• Write a short story incorporating the five elements of literature and narrative devices (e.g., suspense, dialogue, etc.)
• Use the writing process
• Use reading strategies: pause, reread, consult another source, draw upon background knowledge, ask for help
	• Participation in class and small group discussion
	• "Characterization" chart
	• "Sensory Details" web
	• Graphic organizers
	• Short story scored against a rubric
		• Various picture books to illustrate specific elements of literature
		• Student samples of short stories
		• Short story writing guides (see textbook and teacher materials)
		• Short stories from literature textbook and teacher collections:
		  o "Broken Chain" by Gary Soto
		  o "Those Three Wishes" by Judith Gorog
		  o "The Landlady" by Roald Dahl
		  o "In Trouble" by Gary Paulsen
		  o "There Will Come Soft Rains" by Ray Bradbury
		  o "The Circuit" by Francisco Jimeniz
		  o "Charles" by Shirley Jackson
		  o "The Monkey's Paw" by W.W. Jacobs
		  o "The Moustache" by Robert Cormier
		  o "Raymond's Run" by Toni Cade Bambara
		  o "The Tell-Tale Heart" by Edgar Allan Poe
		  o "Rain, Rain Go Away" by Isaac Asimov

McREL STANDARDS		
Writing: • Writes narrative accounts, such as **short stories** (e.g., establishes a situation, plot, persona, point of view, setting, conflict, and resolution; develops complex characters; creates an organizational structure that balances and unifies all narrative aspects of the story; uses a range of strategies and literary devices; reveals a specific theme) • Uses the general skills and strategies of the **writing process:** prewriting, drafting and revising, editing and publishing • Uses the stylistic and rhetorical aspects of writing: **descriptive** language, **paragraph** form; variety of **sentence structure; transitional** devices • Uses **grammatical and mechanical conventions** **Reading:** • Uses reading skills and strategies to understand a variety of literary passages and texts (e.g., short story)	• Knows the defining characteristics of **[fiction] genre** • Understands complex elements of **plot development** (e.g., cause-and-effect relationships; use of climax; development of conflict and resolution) • Understands elements of **character development** (e.g., character traits and motivations; relationships between character and plot development; development of characters; how motivations are revealed) • Understands the **use of language** in literary works to convey mood, images, and meaning (e.g., dialect; dialogue; irony; voice; figurative language; sentence structure; punctuation) • Understands the **effects of an author's style** on the reader • Understands **point of view** in a literary text (e.g., first and third person, limited and omniscient, subjective and objective) • Understands inferred and recurring **themes** in literary work • Makes **connections** between the motives of characters or the causes for complex events in texts and those in his or her own life	

NOTE: Standards and benchmarks are used and/or adapted by permission of McREL. Copyright © 2004, McREL.

Reprinted from *Curriculum Mapping: A Step-by-Step Guide for Creating Curriculum Year Overviews* by Kathy Tuchman Glass. Thousand Oaks, CA: Corwin Press, www.corwinpress.com. Reproduction authorized only for the local school site or nonprofit organization that has purchased this book.

HIGH SCHOOL CURRICULUM YEAR OVERVIEW EXAMPLES

HIGH SCHOOL

Curriculum Year Overview Unit Examples

Two integrated units are mapped in the high school section.

- Figure 4.24: Societal Injustice—*The Crucible* and McCarthyism. This unit merges the study of McCarthyism with Arthur Miller's *The Crucible*. Students explore the historical events of the McCarthy era and compare themes evident in this period in history with the novel.
- Figure 4.25: Perspectives of War: Internment and Atomic Warfare. World War II, Japanese internment and atomic warfare are the focus of this interdisciplinary unit combining language arts, science, and social studies. Students study the political backdrop of World War II, discuss ethical issues related to atomic warfare and internment, examine the science of atomic warfare, and more.

Figure 4.24 Unit: Societal Injustice—*The Crucible* and McCarthyism

UNIT: Societal Injustice—*The Crucible* and McCarthyism—**TIMING:** September
Unit Guiding Questions: 1. How did Puritan society instill fear? **2.** How are individuals affected by society? **3.** Why might Proctor be called a tragic hero? **4.** How is human weakness shown in *The Crucible*? **5.** How do the themes and events in *The Crucible* parallel the McCarthy era? **6.** How do the themes of the play relate to modern social issues? **7.** How has the author's perspective shaped this play?

McREL STANDARDS:	**Skills/Activities:**

Writing
• Uses the general skills and strategies of the writing process
• Uses the stylistic and rhetorical aspects of writing
• Uses grammatical and mechanical conventions in written compositions
 	
Reading
• Uses the general skills and strategies of the reading process
• Uses reading skills and strategies to understand and interpret a variety of literary texts
• Uses reading skills and strategies to understand and interpret a variety of informational texts
	• Write a Response to Literature essay using the writing process steps: prewriting, drafting, revising, editing, publishing
	• Organize the paper for a Response to Literature format; see "Assessment" for specifics of paper content and format
	• Write a variety of sentence types (e.g., simple, compound, complex)
	• Organize ideas to provide cohesion and balance in paper
	• Divide paragraphs appropriately and include transitional words and phrases
	• Write with an understanding of audience and purpose
	• Employ appropriate reading strategies
	• Extrapolate salient points from text
	
	Assessment:
	• Participation in class and small-group discussion
	• Graphic organizers and notes
	• Response to Literature essay scored against rubric that:
	  ○ demonstrates a comprehensive grasp of the significant ideas of literary works;
	  ○ supports important ideas and viewpoints through accurate and detailed references to the text or to other works;
	  ○ demonstrates awareness of the author's use of stylistic devices and an appreciation of the effects created;
	  ○ identifies and assesses the impact of perceived ambiguities, nuances, and complexities within the text.

History • Understands the role of McCarthyism in the early Cold War period (e.g., the rise of McCarthyism, the effect of McCarthyism on civil liberties, and McCarthy's fall from power; the connection between postwar Soviet espionage and internal security and loyalty programs under Truman and Eisenhower)	**Skills:** • Create a timeline • Write a well-balanced, accurate, and insightful essay using proper writing conventions and strategies of the writing process • Employ appropriate reading skills and strategies • Compare/contrast information on the same topic gleaned from many resources **Assessment:** • Annotated timeline about the rise of McCarthyism and McCarthy's fall from power • Analytical essay about the effects of McCarthyism on civil liberties; scored against rubric

Resources: *The Crucible* by Arthur Miller; commentaries on *The Crucible;* social studies textbook; Response to Literature student and published samples; literature textbook as resource for Response to Literature writing; various secondary and primary resources for McCarthyism

NOTE: Standards and benchmarks are used and/or adapted by permission of McREL. Copyright © 2004, McREL.

Reprinted from *Curriculum Mapping: A Step-by-Step Guide for Creating Curriculum Year Overviews* by Kathy Tuchman Glass. Thousand Oaks, CA: Corwin Press. www.corwinpress.com. Reproduction authorized only for the local school site or nonprofit organization that has purchased this book.

Figure 4.25 Unit: Perspectives of War: Internment and Atomic Warfare

---

UNIT: Perspectives of War: Internment and Atomic Warfare—**TIMING:** September

Unit Guiding Questions: 1. Why did the United States drop the bomb on Japan? **2.** How were people affected by the bomb physically and emotionally? **3.** How is an atomic bomb constructed? **4.** How is an atomic bomb viewed in today's political climate? **5.** How is Japan's social and military posture today compared with post–WWII? **6.** How were issues resolved or exacerbated by Japanese internment?

McREL STANDARDS:	Skills:
SCIENCE	• Identify the individuals and their areas of expertise who contributed to creating the atomic bomb
• **Understands the sources and properties of energy:** Knows that nuclear reactions convert a fraction of the mass of interacting particles into energy (fission involves the splitting of a large nucleus into smaller pieces; fusion is the joining of two nuclei at extremely high temperature and pressure) and release much greater amounts of energy than atomic interactions	• Identify and debate sides of various issues
	• Synthesize information from multiple sources and identify the different perspectives found in each medium
• **Understands forces and motion:** Knows that nuclear forces are much stronger than electromagnetic forces, which are vastly stronger than gravitational forces; the strength of nuclear forces explains why great amounts of energy are released from the nuclear reactions in atomic or hydrogen bombs, and in the Sun and other stars	• Structure ideas and arguments in a sustained, persuasive, and sophisticated way and support them with precise and relevant examples
	• Compare/contrast Japan's social and military situation then and now
	• Define nuclear reactions
HISTORY	• Identify the differences between and possible results of nuclear, electromagnetic, and gravitational forces
• Understands events that led to the Japanese attack on Pearl Harbor	
• Understands how World War II influenced the home front (e.g., the effects of the relocation centers on Japanese American families)	**Assessments:**
	• Oral and written description of the events and attitudes leading to the attack on Pearl Harbor
• Understands characteristics of the end of World War II	• Poster explaining the sources and properties of energy that create atomic interactions
WRITING	• Class and small-group participation and discussion
• Uses the general skills and strategies of the writing process	• Reading journal
• Uses the stylistic and rhetorical aspects of writing	• Persuasive essay scored against rubric that:
• Uses grammatical and mechanical conventions in written compositions	o structures ideas and arguments in a sustained and logical fashion;
READING	o uses specific rhetorical devices to support assertions (e.g., appeal to logic through reasoning; appeal to emotion or ethical belief; relate a personal anecdote, case study, or analogy);
• Uses the general skills and strategies of the reading process	
• Uses reading skills and strategies to understand and interpret a variety of literary texts	o clarifies and defends positions with precise and relevant evidence, including facts, expert opinions, quotations, and expressions of commonly accepted beliefs and logical reasoning;
• Uses reading skills and strategies to understand and interpret a variety of informational texts	
LISTENING/SPEAKING	o addresses readers' concerns, counterclaims, biases, and expectations.
• Uses listening and speaking strategies for different purposes	

Resources: *Hiroshima* by John Hersey; *When the Emperor Was Divine* by Julie Otsuka; science and social studies textbooks; primary and secondary source materials; periodic table

---

NOTE: Standards and benchmarks are used and/or adapted by permission of McREL. Copyright © 2004, McREL.

Reprinted from *Curriculum Mapping: A Step-by-Step Guide for Creating Curriculum Year Overviews* by Kathy Tuchman Glass. Thousand Oaks, CA: Corwin Press, www.corwinpress.com. Reproduction authorized only for the local school site or nonprofit organization that has purchased this book.

Computer Software and Continued Professional Success

COMPUTER SOFTWARE PROGRAMS

Curriculum mapping software is an invaluable tool for educators who wish to create and manage a curriculum mapping document. Companies that produce curriculum mapping software are listed on page 106. The software programs are all fairly similar, so it is important to list the specific needs of your teacher group before deciding whether or not software is an option and, if so, which software is optimal.

It is imperative to start with a prescribed process in the area of curriculum mapping, and then utilize the software at any point in the process. In this book, I have set forth a process that is generated on a table in either Microsoft Word or Excel, but a software program could be integrated anywhere in the process. In fact, you could create the document through Step #11, and then employ the computer software company to download all data from Microsoft Word or Excel into their program. Beyond that, you can expand your curriculum mapping capabilities in many ways, such as generating analytical reports, preparing presentations, varying graphic representations of the curriculum map, cross-referencing maps throughout the school or district, and so forth.

Whether or not you use a software tool and at what juncture you use it are secondary to the quality and breadth of professional development incorporated in the process of developing a curriculum map. For example, collaborative conversations about the philosophy, pedagogy, and best practice are crucial, so that teachers can expand their expertise along the way and grow professionally.

To determine if a software tool is right for your group of teachers, I suggest the following procedure using the Worksheet for Computer Software Consideration (Figure 5.1):

- As a group, read the list of criteria in Figure 5.1, and reach agreement on which items are most essential for consideration when purchasing a curriculum mapping software program. Place check marks next to each critical item. If your group has additional questions, record them on the blank lines provided at the bottom of the worksheet.
- Ask for three volunteers from the group to investigate answers to the questions.
- Assign each volunteer one of these companies: The Curriculum Mapper, Rubicon Atlas, or TechPaths. Instruct each volunteer to research his or her assigned company online (see below).
- Ask each volunteer to review the information on the Web site of the targeted company.
- Ask each volunteer to request an online demonstration of the tool. There is typically a link on the company Web site that will allow visitors to request a demo.
- Have volunteers fill in answers to as many questions as possible on the Worksheet for Computer Software Consideration.
- Instruct them to speak on the phone to a sales representative at each assigned company to augment answers to questions on the worksheet. Add additional information on the back of each worksheet.
  - o The Curriculum Mapper:1-800-318-4555; www.curriculummapper.com
  - o Rubicon Atlas: 503-223-7600; www.rubicon.com
  - o TechPaths: 203-452-8076; www.perfpathways.com

- Reconvene as a group and have volunteers share their findings. Together, decide which software company's curriculum mapping tool seems to best suit the group's needs. Invite a sales representative to come if possible, so group members have a chance to ask additional questions and see a presentation. Be sure to invite any decision makers (department heads, administrators) to this meeting as well.

Researching and purchasing a software tool is just one facet. The more difficult task is persuading teachers to actually implement it from year to year to access the software's many features and improve the curriculum map. This might require much hand-holding and validation from different teacher groups to build the software's credibility throughout the school and district. So if your group chooses to purchase curriculum mapping software, encourage them to seek a champion and an alternate to be accountable and to support teachers in using the software so that they adopt it and use it on an ongoing basis. Selecting an alternate is important in the event that the point person changes schools or retires. It would be a shame to spend the money on software and not have it used to its full potential. In short, make sure that there is sponsorship to support implementation of the software in continuous refinement, revision, and reporting of curriculum maps.

CONTINUED PROFESSIONAL SUCCESS

Working with teachers, you expand their expertise as they embark upon the work of creating a Curriculum Year Overview (CYO). Some may have heard of curriculum mapping, as it has been around for a while, but going through the process of generating the document elevates each member's knowledge base in a number of ways. Naturally, they benefit from what they glean as they work through each step. Even the interpersonal aspect of working as a group is a key growth opportunity.

As facilitator, you will undoubtedly grow too. When I work with each group of teachers to build a map, I always learn something novel that broadens the scope of what I can share with the next group. I also educate myself professionally, so that I am continually learning, which in turn helps all the teachers with whom I work.

The more you educate yourself about curriculum mapping through articles, books, Web sites, and conference attendance, even talking to curriculum mapping software suppliers, the more confident you will be in leading a group to create a Curriculum Year Overview. The new knowledge you acquire will undoubtedly yield an explosion of thought and inquiry that will make this project even richer for your teacher-clients. Learning about different approaches and facets of curriculum mapping affords you the broad perspective needed in a leadership position. As mentioned in the Introduction, I suggest you obtain any of the books listed in the Bibliography to further your understanding and knowledge and ensure continued professional success.

Enjoy your journey of working with teachers to create a curriculum map and, in the process of guiding them, expanding your own expertise. This project will enable teachers to approach their jobs with more professionalism, keener insight, clearer vision, and stronger commitment to their work. We are forever seeking ways to help students reach even higher than they thought possible. Students are the fortunate recipients of the growth of this committed group of educators.

Figure 5.1   Worksheet for Computer Software Consideration

Worksheet for Computer Software Consideration		
Necessary Criteria?	**CRITERIA**	**Company Name and Contact Information:**
	1. Cost. Costs for purchasing, running and maintaining software? Ask about fees for: • License? • Yearly maintenance? • Software upgrades included in maintenance? • Discounts?	
	2. Software. • Web-based? • User support? • Software updates? • User security?	
	3. Training. • On-site or at company? • Teachers directly trained or facilitator/teacher group trained? • Length of training? • Cost of training? • Ongoing training needed or provided? • Content of training?	
	4. Usability/Content. • Ease of use of software? • Standard components to include on map? • Ability to add features? • Customization of mapping categories and vocabulary? • Ability to customize format? • Foreign-language capability? • Links to standards? • Other links available (e.g., lessons, reference material, etc.)? • Ease of revision? • Ability to share map with colleagues? • Ability to print map off PC or Mac?	
	5. Reports. • Analytical or reporting tools?	
	6. Other. • •	

Copyright © 2007 by Corwin Press. All rights reserved. Reprinted from *Curriculum Mapping: A Step-by-Step Guide for Creating Curriculum Year Overviews*, by Kathy Tuchman Glass. Thousand Oaks, CA: Corwin Press, www.corwinpress.com. Reproduction authorized only for the local school site or nonprofit organization that has purchased this book.

Resources

Below is a listing and explanation of each figure presented in this section:

- **Figures A, B, and C:** Year-at-a-Glance Templates

The figures listed below are referenced in Step 4: "Sketching the Year-at-a-Glance." Each template provides a panoramic picture or broad overview of your entire year. The monthly units serve to detail what is listed in these "Year-at-a-Glance" pages. You can combine two months, for example September/October or November/December, as seen in many examples.

   o **Figure A: Year-at-a-Glance Template for Multi-Subjects**

   This template is designed for self-contained classroom teachers who teach multiple subjects. Note: There are four pages to this document—September to January on the first two pages; February to June on the second two pages. You can combine two months, for example September/October or November/December, as seen in many examples.

   o **Figure B: Year-at-a-Glance Template for Language Arts**

   This is the same usage as Figure A, but designed for language arts teachers.

   o **Figure C: Blank Year-at-a-Glance Template**

   This template is blank so that it can be adapted for the teacher of any subject. Teachers might consider dividing a subject area into natural subdivisions and devoting each separate line item to these subcategories or strands. For example, science—earth sciences, life sciences, physical sciences, investigation; math—number sense, geometry, statistics, etc.

- **Figure D:** Blank Template for Detailed Month/Unit

This figure is referenced in "Step #5: Beginning the Curriculum Year Overview Monthly Units." These pages represent the monthly units and support the "Year-at-a-Glance."

Resource A

Year-at-a-Glance Template for Multi-Subjects

YEAR-AT-A-GLANCE TEMPLATE FOR MULTI-SUBJECTS

	September	October	November	December	January
Social Studies					
Reading					
Writing Types and Strategies					
Written Grammar/ Conventions					

(Continued)

111

YEAR-AT-A-GLANCE TEMPLATE FOR MULTI-SUBJECTS (Continued)

	September	October	November	December	January
Speaking/Listening					
Math					
Science					
Art					
Formal Assessments					

YEAR-AT-A-GLANCE TEMPLATE FOR MULTI-SUBJECTS

	February	March	April	May	June
Social Studies					
Reading					
Writing Types and Strategies					
Written Grammar/ Conventions					

(Continued)

YEAR-AT-A-GLANCE TEMPLATE FOR MULTI-SUBJECTS (Continued)

	February	March	April	May	June
Speaking/Listening					
Math					
Science					
Art					
Formal Assessments					

114

Resource B

Year-at-a-Glance Template for Language Arts

YEAR-AT-A-GLANCE TEMPLATE FOR LANGUAGE ARTS

	September	October	November	December	January
Reading					
Writing Types and Strategies					
Written Grammar/ Conventions					
Speaking/Listening					

YEAR-AT-A-GLANCE TEMPLATE FOR LANGUAGE ARTS

	February	March	April	May	June
Reading					
Writing Types and Strategies					
Written Grammar/ Conventions					
Speaking/Listening					

Resource C

Year-at-a-Glance Template

YEAR-AT-A-GLANCE TEMPLATE

September	October	November	December	January

(Continued)

YEAR-AT-A-GLANCE TEMPLATE (Continued)

February	March	April	May	June

(Continued)

Resource D

Blank Template for Detailed Month/Unit

BLANK TEMPLATE FOR DETAILED MONTH/UNIT

UNIT: _____

Timing: _____   Grades: _____

Guiding Questions:

1)

2)

3)

4)

5)

SKILLS	ASSESSMENTS	RESOURCES
• • • •	• • • •	• • • •

STANDARDS

Content Area: _____

• • • • • •

Content Area: _____

• • • • • •

Content Area: _____

• • • • • •

Content Area: _____

• • • • • •

Copyright © 2007 by Corwin Press. All rights reserved. Reprinted from *Curriculum Mapping: A Step-by-Step Guide for Creating Curriculum Year Overviews*, by Kathy Tuchman Glass. Thousand Oaks, CA: Corwin Press, www.corwinpress.com. Reproduction authorized only for the local school site or nonprofit organization that has purchased this book.

Bibliography

Clough, D. B., James, T, L., & Witcher, A. E. (1996). Curriculum mapping and instructional supervision. *NASSP Bulletin, 80*(581), 79–83.

Drucker, P. F. (1993). *The Practice of Management.* New York: HarperCollins.

Erickson, L. H. (2002). *Concept-Based Curriculum and Instruction: Teaching Beyond the Facts.* Thousand Oaks, CA: Corwin Press.

Jacobs, H. H. (Ed.). (1997). *Mapping the Big Picture: Integrating Curriculum & Assessment K–12.* Alexandria, VA: Association for Supervision and Curriculum Development.

Jacobs, H. H. (2004). *Getting Results With Curriculum Mapping.* Alexandria, VA: Association for Supervision and Curriculum Development.

Marzano, R. & Kendall, J. (2004). *Content Knowledge: A Compendium of Standards and Benchmarks for K–12 Education,* 4th ed. Aurora: CO: McREL.

McTighe, J. & Wiggins, G. (1998). *Understanding by Design.* Alexandria, VA: Association for Supervision and Curriculum Development.

McTighe, J. & Wiggins, G. (2005). *Understanding by Design,* 2nd Ed. Alexandria, VA: Association for Supervision and Curriculum Development.

Minkel, W. (2002). Charting a clear course. *School Library Journal, 48*(9), 60–61.

North Central Regional Educational Laboratory (2003). Curriculum mapping: A process for continuous quality improvement. *Notes and Reflections,* Issue 4, Spring 2003.

Tomlinson, C. et al. (2001). *The Parallel Curriculum.* Thousand Oaks, CA: Corwin Press.

Tomlinson, C. & McTighe, J. (2006). *Integrating Differentiated Instruction.* Alexandria, VA: Association for Supervision and Curriculum Development.

Udelhofen, S. (2005). *Keys to Curriculum Mapping: Strategies and Tools to Make It Work.* Thousand Oaks, CA: Corwin Press.

West-Christy, J. Roadmap to success: A curriculum mapping primer. *Education Up Close,* July 2003. Retrieved June 22, 2005, from www.glencoe.com/sec/teachingtoday/educationupclose.phtml/35

Content Standards

Education World (access to all state standards) www.education-world.com/standards/state/index.shtml

Mid-continent Research for Education and Learning (McREL): Phone: 303-337-0990; www.mcrel.org/standards-benchmarks/

National Center for History in the Schools (NCHS): Phone: 310-825-4702; www.sscnet.ucla.edu/nchs/

National Center on Educational Outcomes (access to all state standards) http://education.umn.edu/nceo/TopicAreas/Standards/StatesStandards.htm

National Council for the Social Studies (NCSS): Phone: 800-683-0812; www.socialstudies.org/standards/

The National Council of Teachers of English (joint effort with NCTE and International Reading Association (IRA): Phone: 217-328-3870 or 877-369-6283; www.ncte .org/about/over/standards/110846.htm

National Council of Teachers of Mathematics (NCTM): Phone: 703-620-9840; www.nctm.org/standards/

National Science Teachers Association (NSTA): Phone: 703-243-7100; www.nsta .org/standards

Curriculum Mapping Software

The Curriculum Mapper. Westjam Enterprises, Westmont, IL. Retrieved February 7, 2006, from www.curriculummapper.com/homesite/default.htm Phone: 800-318-4555

Eclipse Curriculum Manager. Eclipse Academic Systems LLC, Madison, WI. Retrieved February 7, 2006, from www.eclipseacademic.com/mainweb/home/

Rubicon Atlas. Atlas Management, Portland, OR. Retrieved February 7, 2006, from www.rubiconatlas.com/

TechPaths. TechPaths, Guilford, CT. Retrieved February 7, 2006, from www.perfpath ways.com/

Videotape

Association for Supervision and Curriculum Development (Producer). (1999). *Curriculum mapping: Charting the course for curriculum content.* [Videotape] Available from the Association for Supervision and Curriculum Development, 1703 North Beauregard Street, Alexandria, VA 22311. www.ascd.org

Index

CORWIN PRESS

The Corwin Press logo—a raven striding across an open book—represents the union of courage and learning. Corwin Press is committed to improving education for all learners by publishing books and other professional development resources for those serving the field of PreK–12 education. By providing practical, hands-on materials, Corwin Press continues to carry out the promise of its motto: **"Helping Educators Do Their Work Better."**

2712 Gift